JAPAN TRAVEL GUIDE 2024

YOUR STRESS-FREE TRAVEL WITH PRACTICAL ITINERARIES, LOCAL SECRETS, AND COMPLETE TRANSPORT DETAILS

HANA TAKASHIRO

Dedication

I wrote this guide for people like you, who love the little things: the quiet temples, the bustling markets, and the unexpected moments that make a trip unforgettable. I hope this book helps you find joy in every corner, and that it makes your journey just a little bit easier and a whole lot more fun. Have fun!

COPYRIGHT © 2024 BY HANA TAKASHIRO

First Edition

DISCLAIMER

The information provided in this guidebook is based on the author's personal experiences, research, and opinions. While every effort has been made to ensure the accuracy of the details included, some information may have changed since the time of writing. The author does not guarantee the completeness, reliability, or accuracy of any content within this guide.

The author is not responsible for any errors, omissions, or changes in prices, locations, or services mentioned in the book. Travelers are encouraged to verify important details, such as transport schedules, opening hours, and costs, directly with the relevant service providers before planning their visit.

This guide is meant to offer suggestions and general guidance, but decisions made based on the content of this book are the responsibility of the reader. The author will not be held liable for any loss, damage, or inconvenience arising from the use of the information in this guide.

For updated information or any concerns regarding errors, please contact the author at *hanatakashirotravel2024@gmail.com*

CONTENTS

CHAPTER 1
INTRODUCTION

This guide is all about giving you **exactly what you need**—clear and simple info to help you travel without any stress. You'll find **locations**, **prices**, **how to get around**, and **what to eat**, so you can explore without getting lost in too many details.

I've done my best to make it easy for you, with **tips on the best places to visit**, like **Tokyo's must-see spots**, **Kyoto's famous temples**, and where to grab the best food in **Osaka**. **If you're looking for transportation help**, you'll see how to get from one place to another, whether it's by train, bus, or even walking. **I made sure to include important costs**, so you know exactly what to expect for food, tickets, and transportation.

This guide is small and **straight to the point**, so you can carry it easily and check it whenever you need to. It's designed to save you time and let you focus on enjoying your trip. **No extra stuff, just what's useful**. You'll get around easier, find good food faster, and make the most of every day without having to figure things out on your own. I put together all the essentials, and I hope it helps you have a great time.

The country is made up of four main islands: **Honshu**, **Hokkaido**, **Kyushu**, and **Shikoku**, located near **China**, **South Korea**, and **Russia**. Its geography stretches from snowy mountains in the north to tropical beaches in the south, so you'll experience everything from **cold winters** perfect for skiing in **Hokkaido** to warm, humid summers in places like **Okinawa**. The most popular times to visit are **spring**, when the cherry blossoms bloom and cover cities in pink, and

autumn, when the fall leaves create stunning scenery in areas like **Kyoto** and **Nikko**.

With a population of around **126 million**, the country is known for blending ancient traditions with cutting-edge technology. One moment you might be wandering through a quiet temple in **Kyoto**, and the next, you could be shopping in one of **Tokyo's** futuristic districts filled with high-rise buildings and neon lights. The country's history stretches back thousands of years, once ruled by emperors and **samurai**. Despite modern advancements, you'll find traditions like **tea ceremonies** and **sumo wrestling** remain a strong part of the culture. The influence of local brands like **Sony**, **Nintendo**, and **Toyota** can be felt worldwide, and its pop culture—through **anime**, **manga**, and **video games**—is everywhere today.

Millions of tourists come for the **rich cultural experiences**, the world-class food, and the unique mix of old and new. Whether it's hiking up **Mount Fuji**, exploring bustling cities, or simply indulging in a bowl of fresh **sushi** in **Tokyo's Tsukiji Fish Market**, there's something for everyone. The food alone is a reason to visit, with endless varieties like **ramen**, **soba**, **tempura**, and more. A lot of visitors are drawn by the safe, clean streets, the efficiency of the public transportation, and how easy it is to get around.

Every year, over **30 million tourists** visit, with most staying for **7 to 14 days**. **Tokyo**, **Kyoto**, and **Osaka** are the main draws, each offering something different. **Tokyo** is a vibrant capital with shopping, nightlife, and modern attractions like **Shibuya Crossing**, while **Kyoto** is more traditional, known for its temples, shrines, and **geisha** culture. **Osaka** is famous for its street food and lively atmosphere.

If you're traveling alone, you can expect to spend about ¥10,000 to ¥15,000 per day, which is around **€65-€100** or **$70-$110**, covering basic accommodations, meals, and transportation. Families of four will need a bigger budget, around **¥30,000 to ¥50,000** per day (roughly **€200-€320** or **$220-$350**), depending on where you stay and what activities you choose. Visiting theme parks like **Tokyo Disneyland** or **Universal Studios Japan** will raise the cost, with tickets starting at **¥8,200 per adult**.

The currency used is the **Yen (¥)**. Right now, **¥1,000** equals around **€6.50** or **$7**, and **¥10,000** equals about **€65** or **$70**. Though credit cards are widely accepted in larger cities, it's a good idea to carry cash, especially in smaller towns or rural areas. You can find ATMs in **7-Eleven** and **FamilyMart** convenience stores, which are almost everywhere.

CHAPTER 2
TOKYO

2.1.1 HISTORY

I n the **1600s**, this place was called **Edo**, just a small fishing town, but when **Tokugawa Ieyasu** took control and made Edo his power base, things changed quickly. **The Tokugawa Shogunate** made Edo the center of political power in the country, and while the emperor stayed in Kyoto, real control was in Edo. For over 250 years, during the **Edo Period**, the city became a huge urban center, with a population exploding into one of the largest cities in the world. You had **samurai**, merchants, and craftsmen making the city thrive, with strict rules enforced by the shogunate to keep things in order. Edo was buzzing with activity, and it became the heart of Japan's economy and culture during that time.

By the **mid-1800s**, everything changed fast. **Commodore Perry** and his ships showed up, and Japan, after centuries of being closed off to the outside world, was forced to open up. This led to major changes. The **Meiji Restoration** in **1868** put an end to the shogun's rule, and the emperor moved from Kyoto to Edo, which was now renamed **Tokyo**, or "Eastern Capital." This wasn't just a name change—**modernization** hit hard and fast. You had new railways, telegraph lines, factories, and Western ideas flooding in. The whole city was transforming from a feudal capital into a modern, international city, embracing industry and technology, while still hanging on to some of the old ways.

Things got rough in **1923** with the **Great Kanto Earthquake**—a disaster that leveled much of the city and caused chaos. Tens of thousands of people were

3

killed, and much of Tokyo was left in ruins. But they rebuilt. Then, during **World War II**, Tokyo was hit hard again. In **1945**, the city was heavily bombed, and whole areas were destroyed. After the war, Tokyo was a wreck. But once again, the rebuilding started, and it wasn't just about recovery—it was about becoming something even bigger.

By the **1950s**, Tokyo was leading Japan's **post-war economic miracle**. New factories, high-tech industries, and rapid development completely reshaped the city, and you can imagine how fast things moved. Skyscrapers were going up, highways were being built, and Tokyo became a global hub. The city hosted the **1964 Olympic Games**, showing the world how far it had come in just a few decades, becoming a symbol of **Japan's rise** from destruction to one of the leading economies in the world.

Today, Tokyo is this massive, ultra-modern city, known for its **technology, innovation, and constant motion**, but if you dig just a little beneath the surface, you'll still find traces of its past—those quiet **temples, old neighborhoods**, and traditions that have survived through centuries of change. The city stands today as a mix of **old Edo** and a thriving, modern capital.

2.1.2 NEIGHBORHOODS

Shibuya is where everything moves fast. You'll see crowds of young people, students, and tourists, all navigating the streets like it's the center of the universe. **The famous crossing** is packed with life, and as soon as the lights turn green, it feels like the entire city is moving at once. The energy here is electric—**fashion, music, tech, and trends** all collide. If you're into youth culture and want to dive headfirst into what's hot right now, this is your spot. The shops are full of streetwear, there are underground clubs, and the whole vibe is all about being ahead of the curve.

Over in **Ginza**, everything is polished, sleek, and high-end. This is where you go if you want **upscale shopping**, fine dining, and luxury. The streets feel more refined, with sleek storefronts showcasing **designer brands** like Louis Vuitton, Chanel, and Gucci. It's not just about shopping, though—**Ginza's restaurants** are world-class, from high-end sushi spots to Michelin-starred restaurants. The area is perfect for those who want a taste of elegance, whether it's browsing art galleries or grabbing coffee in one of the quiet, stylish cafés.

Now, **Asakusa**—this is where you'll find **old-school Tokyo**. It's like stepping back in time, and you immediately feel the shift in atmosphere. **Senso-ji Temple** dominates the area, and there's a calmness here despite the crowds. Asakusa is all about **tradition**. You'll see women in **kimonos** strolling by, tiny shops selling traditional sweets, and **narrow alleys** that haven't changed much in decades. If you want a break from the modern chaos and want to experience the **historic side** of the city, Asakusa is the place to go.

For something entirely different, head to **Roppongi**. This neighborhood is known for its **nightlife**, with bars and clubs open until the early morning hours. It's not just about the partying, though—Roppongi is also home to some of the city's most important **modern art galleries** and museums, like the **Mori Art Museum**. You'll find a mix of international visitors and locals, and the vibe changes drastically depending on the time of day. By night, it's all neon lights and action, but by day, it has a sleek, artistic energy.

And then there's **Harajuku**, where everything is loud, colorful, and absolutely wild. This is the birthplace of **Tokyo street fashion**, and the people here express themselves in ways you won't see anywhere else. **Takeshita Street** is packed with shops selling everything from punk clothing to quirky accessories. It's where the **fashion-forward crowd** comes to show off their looks, and it's full of energy, creativity, and everything unexpected. If you want to see the latest in **pop culture**, from fashion to kawaii culture, Harajuku is where you'll feel the pulse of something new.

2.2 MUST-SEE ATTRACTIONS

2.2.1 SHIBUYA CROSSING & HACHIKO STATUE

Shibuya is one of the most recognizable neighborhoods, located in the heart of the city. You can reach it easily by taking the **JR Yamanote Line** or the **Tokyo Metro Ginza Line** and getting off at **Shibuya Station**, one of the busiest train stations in the world. The area is famous for **Shibuya Crossing**, that massive pedestrian scramble you've probably seen in every travel video about the city. When the lights turn green, hundreds of people cross from all directions, making it one of the most iconic and photographed places in the world. You'll want to experience the crossing from different angles—maybe try it first on foot, then find a spot at the **Starbucks Tsutaya** overlooking the intersection for an amazing view.

Shibuya has long been known as a **hub for youth culture**, especially since the 1970s, when it became the center for **fashion and entertainment** for the younger crowd. **Shibuya 109**, a department store just outside the station, has been a landmark for decades, housing floors of trendy clothing shops, perfect for anyone wanting to dive into the latest **Japanese streetwear**. It's open from **10 AM to 9**

PM, so you've got plenty of time to shop. And when you need a break, the streets are filled with **cafés, bars, and ramen shops**, with options ranging from quick bites to gourmet experiences. At night, the neon lights make the whole area come alive, and while Shibuya's vibe is more about shopping and hanging out during the day, it turns into a vibrant spot to explore the nightlife later on.

Next, we head to **Ginza**, the city's high-end shopping district, located on the **Tokyo Metro Ginza Line**—just hop off at **Ginza Station**. It's a sharp contrast to the fast-paced energy of Shibuya. Ginza has been **Japan's luxury shopping district** since the **Meiji Period**, when the government decided to modernize the area, transforming it into a Western-style boulevard lined with **brick buildings**. Today, **Chuo-dori Street** is where you'll find **luxury boutiques** like **Louis Vuitton**, **Gucci**, and **Hermès**, each with sleek storefronts showcasing the latest collections. The area is known for its **refined atmosphere**, and most stores open at **11 AM** and close around **8 PM**, so plan your shopping trip accordingly.

But Ginza isn't just about shopping. It's also home to **some of the best fine dining** in the city. You've got everything from **high-end sushi restaurants** to **Michelin-starred French cuisine**, so if you're a foodie, this is the place to treat yourself. A visit to **Sukiyabashi Jiro**, one of the most famous sushi restaurants in the world, requires a reservation well in advance, but if you're lucky enough to get a seat, you'll experience sushi like never before. Don't forget, though, Ginza can be pricey, so even a simple lunch can cost around ¥3,000 to ¥5,000 ($30 to $50 USD), with dinner reaching much higher prices. If you're visiting on the weekend, **Chuo-dori** turns into a **pedestrian-only zone** from **12 PM to 5 PM**, making it the perfect time for a leisurely stroll through the area.

For a completely different experience, head over to **Asakusa**, located northeast of the city. You can get there easily via the **Tokyo Metro Ginza Line**, getting off at **Asakusa Station**. This is where you'll find the famous **Senso-ji Temple**, the city's oldest and most visited Buddhist temple, dating back to the **7th century**. As you walk up to the temple, you'll pass through the iconic **Kaminarimon (Thunder Gate)**, with its massive red lantern swaying above, welcoming visitors from all over the world. **Nakamise-dori**, the street leading up to the temple, is lined with traditional shops where you can buy **souvenirs, snacks**, and **kimonos**, and the smell of fresh **senbei (rice crackers)** and sweet **taiyaki** will tempt you to try something new.

Senso-ji is open **from sunrise to sunset**, and entry to the temple grounds is free. After you've explored the main temple, head to the **Five-Story Pagoda** and the **Asakusa Shrine**, both part of the same complex. If you're visiting during festivals like **Sanja Matsuri** in May, the area becomes alive with street performances, traditional dances, and food stalls. While in Asakusa, take a cruise down the **Sumida River** for a relaxing view of the city's skyline, or rent a **kimono** and stroll through the **historic district** to get a feel for what life was like in Edo-era Japan.

For nightlife and modern art, **Roppongi** is the place to go. Take the **Hibiya Line** to **Roppongi Station**, and you'll find yourself in an area known for its **nightclubs**, **bars**, and **art galleries**. Roppongi has a reputation for being the go-to spot for a night out, especially among expats and international visitors. Some of the biggest clubs, like **Maharaja** and **V2 Tokyo**, open their doors around **9 PM**, and they stay packed until the early hours of the morning, often charging an entry fee of around ¥3,000 to ¥5,000 ($30 to $50 USD). But Roppongi isn't just about the nightlife. It's also home to the **Mori Art Museum**, located in the towering **Roppongi Hills** complex, which features rotating exhibitions of **modern and contemporary art** from world-renowned artists. The museum is open **from 10 AM to 10 PM**, and admission is typically around ¥1,800 ($18 USD). From the **Mori Tower's observation deck**, you can get some of the best panoramic views of the city, especially at night when the skyline is lit up.

For something completely unique, you'll want to visit **Harajuku**, located on the **JR Yamanote Line** at **Harajuku Station**. This neighborhood is famous for its bold **street fashion** and eclectic energy, particularly along **Takeshita Street**, a narrow pedestrian road filled with boutiques selling everything from **vintage clothes** to **quirky accessories**. It's the birthplace of **kawaii culture**, where you'll see people dressed in everything from **gothic lolita outfits** to **cosplay**. The shops here are small but packed with personality, and you can spend hours exploring everything Harajuku has to offer. If you get hungry, try the iconic **crepes** sold along the street, filled with whipped cream, strawberries, or chocolate.

But Harajuku isn't all about fashion and food—it's also home to one of the city's most serene spots: **Meiji Shrine**. Built in **1920** to honor Emperor **Meiji** and Empress **Shoken**, it's surrounded by a peaceful forest of over 100,000 trees. You can visit the shrine for free, and it's open from **sunrise to sunset**. It's a perfect escape from the fast-paced energy of the city, where you can take a quiet walk and even participate in traditional **Shinto rituals**, like making a wish by writing on an **ema** (wooden plaque) or witnessing a traditional Japanese wedding.

2.2.2 THE IMPERIAL PALACE

The **Imperial Palace** is located in **Chiyoda**, right in the middle of the city, and it's not just a home for the **emperor**—it's a symbol of the country's imperial history. The palace stands on the site of the old **Edo Castle**, which was the seat of power during the **Tokugawa Shogunate**. When the shogunate ended with the **Meiji Restoration** in **1868**, the emperor moved from **Kyoto** to the newly renamed **Tokyo**, and the palace became the center of the new imperial government. Even though the inner grounds are not open to the public except on rare occasions, you can still explore the **East Gardens**, which give you a taste of this important historical site.

To get there, the easiest way is by taking the **Tokyo Metro** to **Otemachi Station** (5-minute walk) or **Tokyo Station** (about 10-15 minutes on foot). The entrance to the **East Gardens** is free, and they're open from **9 AM to 4:30 PM** (or until 5 PM from mid-April to August). In winter, the gardens close a bit earlier, around **4 PM**. The East Gardens are closed on **Mondays** and **Fridays**, so be sure to plan ahead.

As you wander through the **East Gardens**, you'll find that they are a perfect mix of **Japanese traditional landscapes** and more Western-style designs. The gardens sit on the former site of the **inner Edo Castle grounds**, and you can still see the remains of the **castle walls**, **guardhouses**, and even the **foundation of the main tower**, which was destroyed in a fire in the 17th century. The paths take you through manicured lawns, winding stone walkways, and clusters of seasonal flowers. If you're visiting in **spring**, the **cherry blossoms** light up the whole area with color, while in **autumn**, the **maple trees** turn deep reds and oranges, making it one of the best spots in the city to catch the fall foliage.

For some history you can book a **guided tour** through the **Imperial Household Agency** website. The tours are free, but you need to make reservations in advance, and they are available in both English and Japanese. These tours take you to parts of the palace grounds that are not normally open to the public, and they give a deeper look into the role of the **imperial family** and the historical significance of the palace.

A must-see spot just outside the palace grounds is the **Nijubashi Bridge**, a double-arched stone bridge that crosses over the moat. It's one of the most famous views in the area, and you'll often see people stopping here to take photos. The bridge, with the palace gate in the background, is especially beautiful during the early morning or late afternoon when the light softens, making it a perfect time for photography. While you can't cross the bridge, it's a great place to take in the palace's architecture and surrounding scenery.

There are two special days each year—**January 2nd** (New Year's Greeting) and **February 23rd** (the Emperor's Birthday)—when the **inner palace grounds** are open to the public. On these days, thousands of people gather to see the **imperial family**, who make a rare public appearance on the palace balcony. If you're in the city during these dates, it's an amazing opportunity to witness a significant cultural event that few travelers get to experience.

After visiting the palace and the gardens, you can head over to nearby **Kokyo Gaien National Garden**, a large open park with wide lawns and tree-lined paths, perfect for relaxing or picnicking. Another quiet spot worth exploring is **Kitanomaru Park**, just north of the East Gardens, which houses the **Nippon Budokan**, a famous martial arts and concert venue.

2.2.3 MEIJI SHRINE

The shrine, located in **Shibuya**, is only a short walk from **Harajuku Station** on the **JR Yamanote Line** or **Meiji-jingumae Station** on the **Tokyo Metro Chiyoda Line**. Despite being in the heart of the city, once you pass through the towering **torii gate**, you're suddenly surrounded by a peaceful forest of over **100,000 trees**, making you feel like you've left the modern world far behind.

The shrine is dedicated to **Emperor Meiji** and **Empress Shoken**, who were crucial in transforming the country during the **Meiji Restoration** in the late 19th century. The shrine was originally built in **1920** to honor their spirits, but it was destroyed during **World War II** bombings and later rebuilt in **1958**. The architecture reflects traditional **Shinto** simplicity, using cypress wood and designed to blend harmoniously with the natural surroundings.

When you visit, the first thing to do is pass through the **massive torii gate**, which is made of Japanese cypress and stands over 12 meters high. It marks your entrance into a sacred space, where everything is quieter, calmer, and more connected to nature. As you walk down the long gravel pathway toward the main shrine, the forest around you helps to filter out the city noise, making the experience feel almost meditative.

At the main shrine, you'll notice visitors making **Shinto offerings**. It's easy to join in if you'd like. First, toss a small coin (traditionally, **5 yen** is considered lucky) into the offering box, then bow twice, clap your hands twice, and bow again. It's a simple but meaningful ritual that's been practiced for centuries. There's also the opportunity to write your wishes on an **ema**, which are small wooden plaques that you can buy for around ¥500 at the shrine. After writing your prayer or wish on the plaque, you hang it on a special rack with hundreds of others. These ema are later collected and offered in a sacred burning ceremony.

The shrine grounds are open **from sunrise to sunset** every day, and there's no entrance fee, so it's a perfect spot for a peaceful break or spiritual reflection. The forested walk to the shrine takes about **10 to 15 minutes**, but you'll want to take your time, as the journey through the trees is part of the experience. On special days, like **New Year's**, millions of visitors come for **hatsumode**, which is the first prayer of the year. The shrine stays open all night on **New Year's Eve**, and despite the huge crowds, it's an incredible way to experience a centuries-old tradition. If you visit during this time, be prepared for long lines, but also a festive atmosphere.

Throughout the year, the shrine also hosts various **seasonal festivals** where you can witness traditional Shinto ceremonies, music, and dance. One particularly beautiful time to visit is during the **autumn harvest festival**, where you can see performances and sometimes traditional Japanese wedding processions. These processions feature the bride and groom dressed in **elaborate kimonos**, walking slowly under a red umbrella, which is a stunning sight against the backdrop of the shrine's simple architecture and natural surroundings.

Once you've spent time at the shrine, you can also explore the nearby **Meiji Jingu Inner Garden**, which is an additional part of the shrine grounds. This garden is especially beautiful in June, when the **iris flowers** are in full bloom, creating a vibrant display of colors. There's a small fee of **¥500** to enter the garden, but it's worth the visit, especially if you're looking for a quieter spot to reflect.

Getting to **Meiji Shrine** is easy. From **Harajuku Station**, it's just a short walk from the station's **Omotesando Exit**. The shrine is open year-round, but to avoid the larger crowds, it's best to visit either early in the morning or later in the afternoon, especially if you want to enjoy the quiet walk through the forested grounds.

2.2.4 TOKYO SKYTREE

The **Skytree** is located in the **Sumida** district, towering over the city as the tallest structure in the entire country at **634 meters**. It's more than just a tall building;

when you visit, you're going to get one of the **best views in the world**. The **Tembo Deck**, at **350 meters**, is the first observation level where you'll get a complete **360-degree view** of the entire city, from the sea of buildings below to distant landmarks like **Mount Fuji** on clear days. But if you want to go even higher, the **Tembo Galleria** at **450 meters** offers an even more impressive perspective—like you're literally above the city, looking down at everything, which makes you feel like you're floating in the air.

The tower was completed in **2012** and was built primarily as a **broadcasting tower** to support digital TV signals, but it's become one of the most iconic spots in the city. Its design is inspired by **traditional Japanese aesthetics**, combined with cutting-edge technology, making it not only a functional structure but also a symbol of **modern Japan**.

To get the best experience, the **sunset** is the ideal time to visit. As the day turns into night, the view changes completely—the sky glows with shades of orange, purple, and pink, and then, once the sun dips below the horizon, you can watch the entire city light up. The **night view** is just as stunning as the daytime, with the twinkling city lights stretching out endlessly in every direction. You'll see all the famous landmarks, and from this height, everything feels calm and distant, despite the city's busy energy.

At the base of the tower, there's **Skytree Town**, a large shopping and dining complex where you can easily spend a few extra hours. It has **over 300 shops**, selling everything from souvenirs to high-end brands, and there are plenty of restaurants offering a wide range of food, including **traditional Japanese meals** and international dishes. It's a great place to relax before or after heading up the tower. You can even visit **Sumida Aquarium** or the **Konica Minolta Plane-tarium**, both located inside the Skytree Town complex.

The tower is open daily from **9 AM to 9 PM**, and you'll want to plan your visit to avoid the busiest times. **Tickets** to the **Tembo Deck** range from **¥2,100 to ¥3,100**, depending on the time of day and whether you book in advance or at the door. If you want to go all the way up to the **Tembo Galleria**, you'll need to pay an additional **¥1,000**, which is worth it if you're looking for the ultimate view. Booking tickets online is the best way to avoid long lines, especially during peak tourist seasons. The website allows you to select your time slot, so you can skip some of the wait when you arrive.

If you're in the mood for an extra thrill, there's a **glass floor** section on the Tembo Deck, where you can stand directly above the streets, looking straight down through the transparent floor. It's an exhilarating experience, especially if you're not afraid of heights! The Skytree is easy to get to—just take the **Tobu Skytree Line** to **Tokyo Skytree Station**, which drops you off right next to the tower. Alternatively, you can take the **Asakusa Line** to **Oshiage Station**, which is also very close.

2.2.5 AKIHABARA

Akihabara is located in **Taito** and **Chiyoda wards**, and it's easily one of the most famous areas for **electronics, anime, manga, and gaming** culture. To get there, just hop on the **JR Yamanote Line** and get off at **Akihabara Station**. If you're on the **Tokyo Metro Hibiya Line**, you can also stop at **Akihabara Station**, and from either, it's just a short walk into the heart of the district. The streets are lined with massive buildings, all packed with stores and arcades, and every corner feels like it's buzzing with energy, pulling you into the world of **otaku culture**.

Akihabara first gained its reputation as **"Electric Town"** after **World War II**, when it became the go-to place for electronics and radio parts. Over time, as technology advanced, Akihabara evolved into a hub for everything related to **computers, gadgets, and digital devices**. In the late 90s and early 2000s, the district also became deeply connected to **anime, manga**, and **video games**, drawing in fans from all over the world. Today, Akihabara is the place where you can explore everything from **cutting-edge tech** to the most obscure **anime collectibles**.

The area really comes to life around **10 AM**, which is when most of the stores open. Shops stay open until about **8 PM** or **9 PM**, and if you're heading to one of the bigger **game centers** like **SEGA Akihabara**, they're usually open until **11 PM** or even later, so you've got plenty of time to explore everything the district has to offer. The streets are packed during the weekends, so if you want to avoid the crowds, going during a weekday, especially in the morning, is your best bet. There's no entrance fee to wander around the streets and browse the shops, but of course, if you're planning on buying some **anime figures**, **electronics**, or trying out the arcades, it's good to budget for that.

One of the main draws is the huge selection of **anime and manga merchandise**. You'll find massive stores like **Animate** and **Mandarake** that specialize in everything related to **anime culture**. Animate has several floors dedicated to anime goods, from **figures and posters** to **DVDs and Blu-rays** of your favorite shows. If you're into rare and vintage collectibles, **Mandarake** is your spot. This store is like a treasure trove for anime lovers, with **hard-to-find items**, **old manga volumes**, and even **cosplay costumes**. You can get lost for hours here just looking at all the unique things on display.

For **gamers**, Akihabara is legendary. You've got places like **Super Potato**, a retro gamer's paradise, where you'll find shelves lined with **vintage consoles** like the **Famicom** or **Sega Genesis,** as well as old game cartridges that you can't find anywhere else. It's a nostalgia overload, and you can even test out some of the old arcade machines they have in-store. If you're more into modern gaming, there are plenty of shops offering the latest **consoles, VR sets,** and **cutting-edge gaming accessories.**

A huge part of the Akihabara experience is the **arcades.** Multi-story game centers like **SEGA Akihabara** or **Taito Station** are packed with everything from **claw machines** to **rhythm games** and **fighting games.** You can spend hours trying to win prizes like anime figures from the UFO catchers or just test your skills in rhythm games like **Dance Dance Revolution.** Each floor in these arcades offers different types of games, and they're open until late at night, so you can easily pop in and spend time there after a day of shopping.

Another uniquely Akihabara experience is the **maid cafés,** which are a huge part of the district's charm. You walk into a **maid café,** like **Maidreamin** or **@Home Café,** and the waitresses, dressed in **cute maid costumes,** greet you with over-the-top sweetness and call you "master" or "princess," depending on the theme. They serve up food that's often decorated with hearts or cute characters, and the entire experience is interactive, from singing to games with the customers. It's playful and light-hearted, and while it might seem unusual, it's a huge part of the **otaku culture** that Akihabara is known for. Most maid cafés are open from around **11 AM** to **10 PM,** and meals usually cost around **¥1,500 to ¥3,000,** depending on what you order and any additional services like taking a photo with the maids.

Many shops still cater to the **electronics market,** offering everything from computer parts to the latest gadgets. You can find stores that specialize in building custom PCs or selling the newest camera equipment, so if you're a tech lover, you'll feel right at home. Some shops even have floors dedicated to **robotics,** with hobby kits and high-tech robots that can be programmed for all kinds of fun uses. The best part about **Akihabara** is that it's constantly evolving.

2.3 FUN LOCAL EXPERIENCES

2.3.1 GO-KART TOURS IN TOKYO

The **Go-Kart Tours** are located in several key areas around the city, with some of the most popular tour providers based near **Shinagawa, Akihabara**, and **Asakusa**. The tours run all year round, and you can choose from **daytime** or **nighttime experiences**, each giving you a completely different feel of the city. Most tours last between **1 to 3 hours**, depending on the route you pick. To get to these tour start points, you can easily access them via public transport, since all major tour providers are located near **train or metro stations**. For example, if you're starting in Akihabara, the easiest way to get there is to take the **JR Yamanote Line** to **Akihabara Station** and from there, it's usually just a few minutes' walk to the go-kart tour offices.

The tours are priced between **¥8,000 and ¥12,000**, depending on the length of the tour and the company you choose. This usually includes the go-kart rental, the costume, and insurance, but always double-check what's covered when booking. Some companies also offer discounts for larger groups or special rates if you book online in advance. Booking ahead is strongly recommended, especially during peak tourist seasons like **spring** (for cherry blossoms) or **autumn** (for fall foliage), because these tours can fill up fast.

Before you hit the road, you'll need a valid **international driver's license** or a Japanese driver's license, along with your **passport**. Without these, you won't be able to participate, so make sure you have them ready before you head over. The reason they're strict on this is because you'll be driving on public roads, sharing lanes with regular traffic, and following the same rules as any other vehicle on the street. Even though the tours are fun and lighthearted, the safety requirements are there for a reason.

Once you're all set, the guide will give you a detailed briefing on safety and how to drive the karts. You'll get instructions on how to operate the vehicle, how to signal to the group, and how to navigate the streets. The karts themselves are small but very easy to handle, and they're designed to be safe and stable, even on the city's busier roads. They don't go over **50 km/h**, so while you'll feel like you're zooming along, you're always within a controlled and legal speed.

One of the most popular routes takes you past **Shibuya Crossing**, where you'll drive right through the world's busiest intersection, dressed in a fun costume, and trust me, you'll get plenty of smiles and waves from people. There are also tours that take you through **Asakusa**, where you can drive past the famous **Senso-ji Temple**, which feels amazing with the contrast of ancient and modern Japan side by side. The **Tokyo Tower** route is another favorite, where you'll get the chance to stop for photos with the iconic red and white structure in the background, and at night, the tower is lit up beautifully, making for some unforgettable views.

One particularly amazing route takes you across the **Rainbow Bridge**, especially during a night tour. You'll be driving with the city lights reflecting off the water below, and the whole skyline lit up in front of you. Most companies offer a range of routes, so depending on the time of day, you can choose what fits best with your schedule. The nighttime tours, with the city lit up, give a totally different vibe compared to the daytime tours, which allow you to see more of the bustling streets and landmarks in daylight.

In terms of history, these go-kart tours became popular a few years ago as a fun way to experience the city, especially after international tourists started looking for more interactive and engaging tours. The concept of dressing in **Mario Kart-style costumes** was inspired by video games, adding a playful twist to regular city sightseeing. While the costumes and karts draw inspiration from pop culture, the tours themselves follow strict traffic rules and safety measures, ensuring that everyone can have fun while staying safe.

While the main thrill is in driving the karts, don't forget to follow the **safety guidelines**. Stay alert on the roads, be mindful of pedestrians and other vehicles, and listen to your guide. They're there to keep you safe and ensure you get the most out of the experience. It's also smart to bring a light jacket, especially for the nighttime tours, as it can get chilly while you're driving through the open-air streets.

2.3.2 ANIME ART CLASSES

Anime art classes are a great way to step directly into the world of **Japanese anime**, where you get hands-on experience learning how to draw your own characters. These classes are often found in areas that are hubs for anime culture, like **Akihabara**, **Nakano Broadway**, and even parts of **Shinjuku**. Classes are usually held in **anime studios** or **specialty art shops**, places where anime art and culture are alive and thriving, so the setting already puts you in the right creative mood.

To get to these classes, you'll find them conveniently located near major train stations. For example, if you're attending a class in **Akihabara**, just take the **JR Yamanote Line** or the **Hibiya Line** to **Akihabara Station**. From there, it's usually a short walk to the studio or shop offering the class. In **Nakano Broadway**, take the **JR Chuo Line** to **Nakano Station**, and you'll be just steps away from the heart of the anime and collectible scene, where many art classes are offered.

Classes are generally open throughout the day, with many running between

10 AM and 6 PM, making it easy to find a session that fits your schedule. Most classes last about **1 to 2 hours,** which is the perfect amount of time to get a solid lesson without feeling rushed. The price for these classes ranges from **¥3,000 to ¥6,000,** depending on the studio and the complexity of the lesson. The fee typically covers everything you'll need, including **materials,** so you don't have to worry about bringing anything with you—just show up ready to draw. It's a great value, especially when you consider that you're getting direct instruction from people who often work in the industry.

Now, let's get into what you'll actually be doing. Whether you're a **complete beginner** or someone with some drawing experience, the classes are designed to be welcoming for all levels. You'll start by learning the fundamentals of **anime drawing,** such as how to draw faces with the right proportions, how to create expressive eyes, and how to give your characters personality. If you're a total newbie, the instructors will walk you through **basic sketches**—like how to draw a head, place the features, and make your character's expression come alive on the page. For more advanced students, the classes can cover things like **dynamic posing, character movement,** or even working with **shading and perspective** to make your drawings more three-dimensional.

You don't need to bring anything. All the **materials** are provided—pencils, paper, erasers, and any other tools you might need to create your character. This takes a lot of the pressure off, especially if you're traveling and didn't pack art supplies. The whole point is to make the experience as fun and easy as possible, so you can focus entirely on learning and creating.

Many of these classes are held by professionals, including **manga artists** or **anime illustrators,** which means you're not just getting a generic art lesson. You're learning directly from people who have worked in the anime industry, and they often share tips and insider knowledge about how characters are developed in the real world. These aren't just casual art sessions—they're a deep dive into how anime is created, giving you a glimpse into the techniques that make anime characters so expressive and memorable.

If you're in places like **Akihabara,** it's an experience that fits perfectly into the day. You can start the morning by visiting some of the famous **anime and manga shops,** grabbing collectibles, and then heading to an anime art class in the afternoon. Some of these studios also offer **themed classes,** where you can learn how to draw in the style of popular anime series, or even recreate characters from famous shows. It's not just about creating a character from scratch, but understanding the styles of different anime genres. These classes can also include learning to draw **chibi characters** (those cute, small-bodied characters with big heads) or learning how to sketch **action poses** for more dynamic scenes.

The history behind these classes ties back to the larger history of **manga and anime** in Japan. Drawing is an integral part of **Japanese pop culture**, and many artists start young, learning how to sketch their favorite characters before going on to create their own. The idea of teaching anime drawing in studios or shops grew from the deep passion for manga and anime that's ingrained in the culture here. When you finish, you'll not only walk away with your very own **hand-drawn anime character**, but you'll also have gained real skills that you can continue to use and improve upon. And the best part? You've done it in the middle of the very culture that invented anime, making it a truly unique and meaningful experience.

2.3.3 THEMED CAFÉS IN TOKYO

For **themed cafés**, you'll find them scattered across key districts like **Akihabara**, **Shibuya**, and **Shinjuku**. These are the go-to areas where **anime culture**, **quirkiness**, and **unique experiences** blend perfectly with food and fun. Getting there is easy because most of these locations are close to major train stations, making them super accessible, especially if you're exploring the city.

Let's start with **cat cafés**. These cafés are found in places like **Shibuya** and **Harajuku**, both well-known for their laid-back, trendy atmospheres. You can reach them by taking the **JR Yamanote Line** to **Shibuya Station** or **Harajuku Station**, and from there it's a quick walk to some of the most popular spots like **MoCHA Cat Café**. These cafés generally open around **10 AM** and stay open until **8 PM**, so you have plenty of time to relax with a cup of tea and enjoy the company of the cats. Expect to pay around **¥1,000 to ¥1,500** for an hour, which usually includes a drink. Some places even offer snacks for the cats that you can feed them, which gives you a little more interaction.

Maid cafés are a whole different world, and **Akihabara** is the heart of this experience. Akihabara is known as the epicenter of **otaku culture**, where everything from **anime** to **video games** comes to life. Just take the **JR Yamanote Line** to **Akihabara Station**, and you'll find streets filled with shops, arcades, and themed cafés. Popular maid cafés like **@Home Café** or **Maidreamin** are usually open from **11 AM to 10 PM**, making them a perfect stop in the middle of your day or after a busy day of exploring. When you walk in, there's often a **cover charge** of around **¥500 to ¥1,000**, and then the food and drinks cost between **¥1,500 to ¥3,000** depending on what you order. It's important to follow the café's etiquette—while the maids are there to create a fun and interactive experience, there are rules about not touching the staff, and photos of the maids are only allowed if you pay for a special photo session.

Robot Restaurant is in **Shinjuku's Kabukicho** area, which is known for its vibrant nightlife and entertainment. To get there, take the **JR Yamanote Line** to **Shinjuku Station**, and from there it's a 10-minute walk to the heart of Kabuki-cho. The Robot Restaurant isn't so much a restaurant in the traditional sense as it is an **insane performance venue** where you'll be treated to a show of **giant robots, flashing lights, loud music**, and over-the-top entertainment. It's an immersive, futuristic spectacle that feels more like a wild concert than a dining experience. The show runs three to four times a day, usually around **5 PM, 7 PM, and 9 PM**, with each performance lasting about **90 minutes**. The price is around **¥8,000** for the full experience, including the show and a simple meal—usually a bento box. It's not the food you're there for, though; it's the **wild ride** that comes with it.

Themed cafés have their roots in **Japanese pop culture. Cat cafés** started popping up in the early 2000s, offering people a place to relax while interacting with cats in an urban setting where owning pets might be difficult. They became a hit because they offered a peaceful break from the busy city life, and the concept spread across the country. As for **maid cafés**, they first appeared in **Akihabara** in the late 1990s, becoming popular with **anime fans and gamers** who wanted to step into a world that felt like a live-action anime. The **Robot Restaurant**, which opened more recently in 2012, was designed to capture the essence of modern **Japanese technology**, mixed with a dose of pure entertainment. Each of these themed cafés reflects a different side of the country's playful, creative spirit.

2.4 PRACTICAL TRAVEL TIPS

2.4.1 HOW TO GET AROUND

When you're figuring out how to get around, it's all about knowing the key transport lines and how to navigate them. The most important one is the **JR Yamanote Line**. This line is like the backbone of the city's train network. It forms a loop and connects major areas like **Shibuya**, **Shinjuku**, **Ueno**, **Ikebukuro**, and **Akihabara**, among others. This means you can easily get to most of the top tourist spots by simply hopping on the Yamanote Line. To reach it, head to any of the big stations, which are everywhere—**Tokyo Station** is a central hub, and from there, you can catch the Yamanote to just about anywhere.

The **Yamanote Line** runs from **around 5 AM until midnight**, so if you're out past midnight, you'll need to plan differently. The price for a single trip on the Yamanote varies depending on how far you go, but generally it's around **¥140 to ¥200**. Using a **Suica** or **Pasmo** card makes things easier because you don't have to buy a ticket every time. You can get these cards from machines in any station, load them up with money, and just tap at the gates to enter and exit. It saves you a ton of time and hassle, and you can also use these cards at **convenience stores**, vending machines, and even some restaurants. Suica and Pasmo cards cost ¥2,000 to buy initially, with ¥500 as a deposit and ¥1,500 loaded on the card to use right away.

Besides the Yamanote, the **subway system** is massive but well-organized. The two main operators are **Tokyo Metro** and **Toei Subway**, and between them, they cover pretty much the whole city. The **Ginza Line** and **Hibiya Line** are some of the more popular ones that you'll use. The **Ginza Line** is great for getting from **Shibuya** to **Asakusa**, hitting popular spots like **Ginza** and **Omotesando** on the way. The **Hibiya Line** takes you to places like **Roppongi** and **Tsukiji**. Both systems are color-coded, and the signs are in both Japanese and English, so even if it looks complicated at first, it's easy to figure out after a couple of rides. The subways run from around **5 AM to midnight**, with fares starting at **¥170**, depending on the distance.

For **bike rentals**, a growing number of neighborhoods have rental services, and it's a fantastic way to explore quieter areas. You'll find bike rental stations in places like **Yanaka**, **Nakameguro**, and **Asakusa**. Renting a bike can cost anywhere from **¥200 to ¥500 per hour**, or around **¥1,500 for a full day**. You can usually find rental shops near parks, river paths, and scenic neighborhoods where biking is a relaxing way to see the sights. A popular route is cycling along the **Meguro River** during cherry blossom season or through the old streets of Yanaka, where you can stop at local shops and cafes. Now, when it comes to **taxis**, they're clean and convenient, especially late at night when the trains stop. But they're not cheap, particularly after **10 PM**, when the rates go up. The base fare is around **¥420 to ¥500** for the first kilometer, and it climbs fast, especially if you're going a long distance. If you're stuck late at night or have too many bags to carry, taxis are a comfortable option, but be ready for the meter to rise quickly. They're great for short distances, but for longer trips across the city, public transport will be a lot cheaper. A little history: the **Yamanote Line** has been around since **1885**, evolving into the loop line we know today. It was originally built to connect the districts around central Tokyo, and as the city expanded, so did the line, becoming one of the busiest and most essential routes for commuters and tourists alike. The **subway system**, on the other hand, started in **1927**, with the **Ginza Line** being the first subway line in Japan—and in all of Asia. It was inspired by the metro systems in cities like London and New York and has since grown into one of the most efficient underground networks in the world.

2.4.2 WHERE TO STAY

Shinjuku is the ultimate spot for nightlife, energy, and convenience. For sure! This district is located on the western side of the city and is one of the busiest areas, known for its neon-lit streets and endless options for dining and entertainment. The easiest way to get here is through **Shinjuku Station**, which is a major transport hub connecting the **JR Yamanote Line, Chuo Line**, and several metro lines. Shinjuku Station is open from **around 5 AM to midnight**, so getting back late at night won't be a problem as long as you're inside that window. Well, where to stay? Shinjuku has everything from budget options like **capsule hotels** to high-end luxury hotels. For a **capsule hotel**, you're looking at around **¥2,500 to ¥5,000 per night**, and they're usually compact but clean and modern. One great choice is **Nine Hours Shinjuku**, a minimalist, space-age capsule hotel perfect if you just need a place to sleep. On the other end of the spectrum, if you want to splurge, you've got **Park Hyatt Tokyo**, famous for its role in the movie *Lost in Translation*. Staying here will cost you upwards of **¥60,000 per night**, but the views from the high floors, the incredible service, and the luxurious rooms make it worth it.

Shibuya is another top spot, especially if you're into **youth culture, fashion**, and want to be in the middle of the action. Shibuya is easily reached by taking the **JR Yamanote Line** to **Shibuya Station**, which is one of the busiest stations in the country. It's also connected to the **Ginza Line, Hanzomon Line**, and **Fukutoshin Line**, making it super easy to get around. Shibuya is known for the famous **Shibuya Crossing**, where thousands of people cross the street at once, and it's the epicenter of trendsetting shops, youth culture, and non-stop energy. Most of the budget-friendly options here are **hostels** or **mid-range hotels**, and prices for budget stays range from **¥3,000 to ¥6,000** per night. If you're looking for a solid, mid-range hotel in Shibuya, **Shibuya Granbell Hotel** is modern, comfortable, and close to the station, with prices starting around **¥12,000 per night**. Shibuya also has a lot of **Airbnb options**, from cozy studios to stylish apartments, and these can be a good choice if you're staying longer.

For a **quieter, more traditional stay**, Asakusa is where you want to be. Located in the northeast part of the city, Asakusa is home to the historic **Senso-ji Temple**, one of the oldest and most significant temples. Staying here gives you a taste of what the city used to be like, with its old streets and laid-back atmosphere. To get here, take the **Ginza Line** or the **Asakusa Line** to **Asakusa Station**. Most of the places to stay in Asakusa are **ryokan** or small, traditional inns. If you want the full experience, book a room at **Ryokan Asakusa Shigetsu**. Rooms here start at **¥8,000 to ¥10,000 per night**, and you'll get to sleep on tatami mats, use futons, and enjoy a traditional Japanese breakfast. It's a simple, authentic experience that gives you a break from the fast pace of the more modern parts of the city.

If you're into **anime, manga,** and all things **pop culture,** then staying in **Akihabara** might be right up your alley. Akihabara is known for its endless shops dedicated to electronics, anime, and gaming. You can get to Akihabara via the **JR Yamanote Line, Keihin-Tohoku Line,** or the **Tokyo Metro Hibiya Line.** The area itself isn't as packed with luxury hotels, but it has a good range of **capsule hotels** and quirky, budget options. If you're looking for something unique, try **Akihabara Bay Hotel,** which is a capsule hotel exclusively for women. It's super clean, affordable, and located right in the middle of the action, with prices starting around **¥3,000 per night.** It's perfect for solo female travelers who want to be in the heart of the anime scene.

For something **luxurious** with traditional touches, you can stay in **Hoshinoya Tokyo,** located in **Otemachi,** just a short walk from the Imperial Palace. This luxury ryokan blends modern amenities with traditional design, offering you a tranquil escape right in the middle of the city. Rooms are spacious, with tatami floors and futons, and they offer **onsen baths** as well. Prices start around **¥90,000 per night,** making it one of the more high-end experiences, but it's ideal if you want to experience top-tier **omotenashi,** the Japanese concept of hospitality.

If you want to stay in a neighborhood with a more **bohemian** and local vibe, try **Nakameguro** or **Shimokitazawa.** These areas are more laid-back and have a creative, artsy feel, filled with small cafes, vintage shops, and galleries. Nakameguro is especially beautiful in spring, when the cherry blossoms bloom along the **Meguro River,** and there are lots of great **Airbnb** options here. You'll find cozy apartments starting around **¥7,000 per night,** perfect if you're staying a bit longer and want to live like a local.

2.5 HIDDEN GEMS

2.5.1 GOLDEN GAI

Golden Gai is located in **Shinjuku,** tucked away near the famous **Kabukicho** area, which is known for its vibrant nightlife. To get there, the easiest way is by taking the **JR Yamanote Line** or the **Tokyo Metro Marunouchi Line** to **Shinjuku Station.** From the station's **East Exit,** it's just a 10-minute walk. The streets leading to Golden Gai might seem narrow and easy to miss, but that's part of its hidden charm. You'll find it nestled between the busy streets, hidden in plain sight, almost as if it's a secret only known by those in the know.

Golden Gai is a **nighttime spot**, with most bars opening around **7 PM** and staying open until the early hours of the morning, typically closing around **2 AM** or even later, depending on the bar and how busy it is. The best time to go is after **9 PM**, when the tiny streets come to life, filled with glowing lights from the bars, soft chatter, and the clinking of glasses. It's not as wild or loud as the rest of Shinjuku's nightlife, but that's what makes it special—it's intimate, cozy, and a little more laid-back, even though it's right in the heart of one of the busiest districts.

As for the **costs**, you'll typically spend **¥500 to ¥1,000** for a drink in most bars. However, some bars will ask for a **cover charge**, usually around **¥500 to ¥1,000** on top of what you pay for drinks. This charge helps support these small, often family-run businesses, especially since the bars are tiny and only seat **five to ten people** at most. Not all bars have this charge, so if you're looking to avoid it, just check for signs outside or ask before stepping in. Many of the smaller, more regular-focused bars tend to have a cover charge, while others are more open to visitors and may skip it. Even if there's a charge, the experience of being in such a unique, atmospheric place makes it worth the extra yen. The history is part of what makes it so fascinating. The area originally developed as a black market after **World War II**, and over the decades, it became a gathering spot for **writers, artists, musicians**, and all kinds of creative people who were drawn to its underground, almost rebellious atmosphere. Despite the rapid development of Shinjuku, **Golden Gai survived**, holding onto its post-war charm while the rest of the city modernized around it. The narrow alleys and wooden buildings you see today are almost unchanged, giving the area a sense of authenticity that you won't find in other nightlife districts. The fact that it hasn't been bulldozed for high-rise buildings is a small miracle, making it one of the last remaining areas of **old Shinjuku**.

When you visit, the main thing to do is **bar-hop**. You'll find that each bar has its own personality. Some are themed around **music genres**, others focus on **film** or even **political conversations**. What's fun is how no two bars are the same—you might start the night in a jazz bar filled with old records, then move to a place decked out with rock-and-roll memorabilia, or a quiet spot where the walls are covered with movie posters. The bartenders are often the owners, and the regulars give each bar a distinct vibe. If you're lucky, you might even stumble into a conversation with a local or find yourself in a tiny bar where people are discussing art or philosophy over drinks.

2.5.2 YANAKA DISTRICT

Yanaka is in the northeastern part of the city, close to **Ueno**. To get there, take the **JR Yamanote Line** and get off at **Nippori Station**. From the station, it's just a **10-minute walk**. The area feels like it's frozen in time, with old streets, wooden buildings, and small shops that give it a traditional atmosphere. This part of the city survived World War II, so it keeps that old-town vibe.

If you visit Yanaka, the best time to go is during the day, around **10 AM to 5 PM**, when the shops and cafes are open. This isn't a place for nightlife; it's all about exploring in the daytime. Walk along **Yanaka Ginza**, the main shopping street, where you'll find **traditional sweets** like **taiyaki** (fish-shaped pastries filled with sweet red bean paste) and **manju** (steamed buns with different fillings), usually costing about **¥150 to ¥200**. The shops here are small and family-run, and you can watch the owners make the sweets right in front of you. The street also has plenty of cute, **cat-themed items** because the area is known for its friendly stray cats.

There are also **handcrafted items** like ceramics and traditional brushes being sold in small galleries and workshops. If you like art or handmade goods, this is a good place to find something unique. While you're there, take a quiet walk through **Yanaka Cemetery**, especially during the **cherry blossom season** in spring, when the trees are full of flowers. It's a peaceful place and home to **Tokugawa Yoshinobu's** grave, the last shogun of Japan.

Yanaka is known for being a calm. The streets are perfect for wandering, and you'll find hidden **temples and shrines** along the way. Unlike the big tourist spots, these temples are small, quiet, and open to everyone. Most places don't have entry fees, but they appreciate donations if you want to give. There's no rush in Yanaka. It's all about **walking around**, trying local treats, and taking in the **slow pace** of life. If you're looking for a break from the busy city, Yanaka is where you can relax and enjoy the **old, traditional side** that's still very much alive.

2.5.3 SECRET ROOFTOP GARDENS

One of the most well-known is the **Shibuya Hikarie rooftop garden**, located on top of the **Shibuya Hikarie** building. To reach it, you just need to take the **JR Yamanote Line** or **Tokyo Metro** to **Shibuya Station** and follow the signs to Shibuya Hikarie. Once you're inside the building, you can take the elevator up to the garden on the 11th floor. It's open daily from **10 AM to 8 PM**, and it's completely **free**. You'll find this rooftop space offers a mix of plants and a calm setting, giving you a break from the bustling streets below, like **Shibuya Crossing**, which is one of the busiest intersections in the city. It's a great place to sit on one of the benches and relax with a drink or snack while watching the city skyline.

In **Ginza**, you can head to the **Tokyu Plaza Ginza** rooftop, which has a modern, polished feel that matches the area's upscale vibe. This garden is located on the **6th floor** of the department store, and the easiest way to get there is by taking the **Tokyo Metro Ginza Line** to **Ginza Station** and walking a few minutes to the plaza. Open from **11 AM to 9 PM**, it's also free to visit and offers a mix of greenery with views of the elegant Ginza district below. It's perfect for relaxing after shopping or just taking a break from the more luxurious side of the city. There's also a **Starbucks** up there, so you can grab a coffee and enjoy it while sitting in the garden, making it an ideal stop during the day.

In **Shinjuku**, head to the **Isetan Department Store** rooftop, which is located on top of the main Isetan building in **Shinjuku-sanchome**. It's only a few minutes' walk from **Shinjuku Station**, and you can reach it by taking the **Tokyo Metro Marunouchi Line** or the **JR Yamanote Line** to the station. The rooftop garden here opens from **10:30 AM to 7 PM**, and like the others, it's free to enter. This garden is special because it often changes with the seasons—during spring, you'll see beautiful cherry blossoms, and in the fall, the trees turn golden and red, offering a perfect spot to sit and relax. The garden also sometimes hosts **seasonal events** or small markets, which adds to its charm.

Most of these rooftop gardens change with the seasons, offering something different each time you visit. In **spring**, the gardens often feature cherry blossoms or other colorful flowers, making them perfect for taking a quiet moment to appreciate the beauty without dealing with large crowds like at popular parks. In **autumn**, the leaves turn bright shades of red, orange, and gold, giving you a peaceful place to enjoy the seasonal change. Even in **winter**, many of these gardens remain open, offering a serene spot to escape the cold streets below. Many of these gardens have **benches**, and some have small seating areas where you can enjoy a coffee or a snack. The best part is how accessible they are, right on top of buildings you might already be visiting for shopping or sightseeing.

Historically, these gardens were designed to provide a **green escape** in the middle of the city. With space at a premium, adding green areas on rooftops became a way to incorporate nature into the urban landscape. These rooftop gardens have been growing in popularity as more people look for quieter spots away from the busy streets, and they're now some of the best-kept secrets in the city for those in the know.

2.6 PRACTICAL INFO

2.6.1 ATTRACTION PRICES & FREE ALTERNATIVES

Meiji Shrine, located right near **Harajuku Station** on the **JR Yamanote Line**, is completely free to enter and is open from **sunrise to sunset**. It's a peaceful retreat in the middle of a huge forest, and you can walk through the **torii gates**, explore the quiet paths, and visit the inner shrine without paying anything. This shrine, dedicated to Emperor Meiji and Empress Shoken, was completed in **1920**, and while the original structure was destroyed during World War II, it was rebuilt in **1958**. It's one of the most important Shinto shrines, so you're getting a real glimpse into the country's cultural and spiritual heart.

Another free gem is **Senso-ji Temple**, located in **Asakusa**. You can easily get there by taking the **Ginza Line** to **Asakusa Station**, and it's just a short walk from the station. This temple is the oldest in the city, dating back to **645 AD**, and it's one of the most popular spots to visit. The grounds are open 24 hours, though the **main hall** itself is open from **6 AM to 5 PM**. You can walk around the temple grounds, enjoy the beautiful architecture, and visit the beautiful **Nakamise Shopping Street** nearby, where you'll find traditional snacks and souvenirs. The best part? It's all free.

Yoyogi Park is another great free spot. Located right next to Meiji Shrine, it's perfect for a quiet walk, a picnic, or just relaxing under the trees. The park is open from **5 AM to 8 PM**, and it's a popular spot for both locals and visitors. In spring, you'll catch the **cherry blossoms**, and it's a great place to experience the changing seasons without spending a dime.

Now, let's talk about **paid attractions** and how you can save money on those. For anyone planning to visit a lot of **museums**, the **Grutto Pass** is your best friend. It costs around **¥2,500** and gives you access or discounts to over **90 museums** and cultural sites, including the **Tokyo National Museum**, **Ueno Zoo**, and the **Edo-Tokyo Museum**. You can buy it at participating museums or online, and it's valid for two months, making it perfect if you plan on visiting multiple spots.

If the **Skytree** is on your list, there's a way to save there, too. The **Skytree combo ticket** includes both the **observation deck** and the **Sumida Aquarium**, and costs around **¥3,100**. This is cheaper than buying each ticket separately, so if you're planning to do both, this is a great deal. The Skytree is open from **9 AM to 9 PM**, and the earlier you go, the better. Not only do you avoid crowds, but the prices can be cheaper if you visit during **off-peak hours**, especially if you book online in advance. You get a bird's-eye view of the entire city, and on clear days, you can even see **Mount Fuji** in the distance.

Another way to save money is to visit attractions during **off-peak times**. Many places offer lower prices if you visit early in the morning or later in the evening. For example, going to the **Tokyo Skytree** or **museums** in the first hour of opening or closer to closing time will help you avoid the big crowds, and some places offer discounts during these times. The same applies to places like **teamLab Borderless**—if you're visiting one of the city's popular interactive museums, always check the website for off-peak tickets. By mixing these **free attractions** like **temples** and **gardens** with **discount passes** and well-timed visits to paid spots, you'll be able to experience so much more without worrying about overspending.

2.6.2 BEST TIMES TO VISIT TOP ATTRACTIONS

The **Tokyo Skytree** as i told you before, one of the tallest towers in the world, is a must-see, and the key to a good visit is getting there either **early in the morning** or **late in the evening**. The Skytree opens at **9 AM**, and the best time to visit is right when it opens to avoid the crowds that start packing in around **noon**. If mornings aren't your thing, head there in the **evening** before it closes at **9 PM**. The tickets are about **¥2,100 to ¥3,100**, depending on the deck you want to visit.

You'll get a stunning view of the entire city, and if you visit on a clear day, you can even see **Mount Fuji**. It's located in **Sumida**, and you can easily get there by taking the **Tobu Skytree Line** to **Tokyo Skytree Station**, or the **Hanzomon Line** to **Oshiage Station**. The observation deck offers breathtaking views whether you go during the day or at night, but the **evening view** with all the city lights is something else.

During **spring, cherry blossoms** are the main attraction, and they bring in huge crowds. Popular spots like **Ueno Park** and **Shinjuku Gyoen** are packed by mid-morning, so the best time to visit is around **7 or 8 AM**. Both parks are easy to reach—**Ueno Park** is right next to **Ueno Station** on the **JR Yamanote Line**, and **Shinjuku Gyoen** is a short walk from **Shinjuku Station** (also on the JR Yamanote Line). These parks are open from **9 AM to 4:30 PM**, and **Shinjuku Gyoen** has a small entry fee of **¥500**, but **Ueno Park** is free. Walking under the blooming cherry trees with hardly anyone around makes the early start worth it, and you'll get the best photos in the morning light.

In **autumn**, when the leaves turn vibrant shades of red and orange, places like **Koishikawa Korakuen Garden** or the **Outer Garden of Meiji Shrine** are the best for leaf-peeping. Again, the trick is to arrive right when they open to enjoy the colors without the crowds. **Koishikawa Korakuen** is located in **Bunkyo** and can be reached via the **Toei Oedo Line** or **Marunouchi Line** to **Korakuen Station**. It's open from **9 AM to 5 PM** and has an entry fee of **¥300**. The **Outer Garden of Meiji Shrine** is near **Harajuku Station** (JR Yamanote Line), and this area is free to explore, with beautiful paths and seasonal displays of flowers and autumn leaves.

For **temples** and **shrines**, the best time to visit is always **early in the morning**. **Senso-ji Temple** in **Asakusa** is open 24 hours, but to experience its serenity, you'll want to visit at **6 or 7 AM**, when the main hall opens and before the crowds arrive. Getting to **Asakusa** is easy—just take the **Ginza Line** or the **Toei Asakusa Line** to **Asakusa Station**. **Meiji Shrine** in **Shibuya**, near **Harajuku Station**, is another spot where the early mornings are the most peaceful. The shrine opens at **5 AM** and stays open until sunset. Entry is free, and you can take your time walking through the forested paths leading up to the shrine before the tourists start pouring in later in the day.

Timing your visit around **local holidays** is important, too. During **Golden Week** (from late April to early May), attractions can get extremely busy with both tourists and locals, so if you happen to be here during this time, plan to visit early or late to avoid the crowds. **Obon**, a holiday in mid-August, is quieter because many locals leave the city to visit family, so that's actually a good time to explore usually crowded spots like **Shibuya Crossing** or **Asakusa** with fewer people around.

CHAPTER 3
KYOTO

3.1 OVERVIEW

T his city, the **cultural capital** of Japan, have alot of history and tradition at every turn, and you can feel it the moment you arrive. Most of the temples, shrines, and historic landmarks are clustered in different parts of the city, making it easy to visit multiple places in one day, and each area has its own story to tell.

For example, if you start your day at **Kinkaku-ji**, or the **Golden Pavilion**, you'll be visiting one of the city's most iconic sites. This **Zen Buddhist temple** is covered in gold leaf and sits next to a reflective pond, creating a view that's famous worldwide. Located in the **northern part** of the city, you can easily reach Kinkaku-ji by taking **Bus 101** from **Kyoto Station**, which takes about 40 minutes. The temple opens daily from **9 AM to 5 PM**, and the **entrance fee** is ¥400. You'll want to go early to avoid the crowds, as this is one of the most popular places for tourists. Walking around the temple grounds, especially in the early morning when the light reflects off the gold, is an experience you won't forget. In every season, from cherry blossoms in the spring to snow in the winter, Kinkaku-ji's beauty changes but never fades.

Another key spot is **Ryoan-ji**, which is famous for its **Zen rock garden**. This simple but profound garden consists of 15 carefully placed rocks surrounded by white gravel that is raked into patterns. It's meant to be a space for meditation and reflection, and the idea is to sit quietly, let your mind clear, and contemplate the garden's simplicity. Located about a 15-minute walk from Kinkaku-ji, it's easy to visit both in one trip. Ryoan-ji is open from **8 AM to 5 PM** (from **8:30 AM in winter**), and the entrance fee is ¥500. The rock garden dates back to the late **15th century** and is considered one of the finest examples of **Zen art** in the country. To get the most out of your visit, try to arrive early or late in the day when the garden is quieter, and you'll have more space to sit and reflect.

If you're interested in the city's **imperial history**, then **Nijo Castle** is a must-see. Built in **1603** as the residence of the **Tokugawa shoguns**, this castle is a symbol of Japan's feudal past and offers a deep dive into the political history of the country. Located in **central Kyoto**, it's about a 20-minute bus ride from Kyoto Station or a short walk from **Nijojo-mae Station** on the **Tozai subway line**. Nijo Castle is open from **8:45 AM to 5 PM**, and admission costs ¥620. As you walk through the castle's corridors, you'll notice the famous **nightingale floors**, which were designed to chirp like birds when walked upon, to prevent intruders from sneaking in unnoticed. The castle's gardens, which are especially beautiful during **cherry blossom season** and **autumn**, are perfect for a peaceful stroll after exploring the historic rooms inside.

For a more spiritual experience, visit **Fushimi Inari Shrine**, located at the base of **Mount Inari** in the southern part of the city. This shrine is famous for its thousands of **bright red torii gates**, which form a stunning pathway that leads up the mountain. It's dedicated to **Inari**, the Shinto god of rice, and is one of the most important shrines in Japan. Fushimi Inari is open 24 hours a day, and admission is free, so you can visit at any time, but it's best to go early in the morning or late in the evening to avoid the crowds. The entire hike to the top of the mountain takes about **2-3 hours**, but even walking through the lower sections of the gates is an unforgettable experience. The shrine is a short walk from **Inari Station** on the **JR Nara Line**, only five minutes from Kyoto Station.

If you're interested in the origins of the **tea ceremony**, then make sure to visit the **Daitoku-ji Temple complex**, where **Sen no Rikyu**, the master of tea, practiced and taught this ancient art. Daitoku-ji is located in the northern part of the city, and it's a 10-minute bus ride from **Kitaoji Station** on the **Karasuma subway line**. The complex consists of multiple sub-temples, each with its own gardens and tea rooms, offering a quiet, reflective atmosphere. Open from **9 AM to 4:30 PM**, each sub-temple may have its own entrance fee, usually around ¥400-¥600. The temple grounds are quieter and less crowded than many of the other big attractions, making it a great place to relax and experience a more intimate side of **Zen culture**.

3.1.2 BEST AREAS TO STAY

Gion offer a traditional experience and has been the **center of geisha culture** for centuries, and today it remains one of the few places in Japan where you can still catch a glimpse of **geishas and maikos (apprentice geishas)** heading to their evening appointments. The streets are narrow, lined with **old wooden machiya houses**, some of which date back hundreds of years. This area is particularly beautiful in the evening, when the streets are lit by lanterns, giving it a timeless feel.

To get to Gion, you can take the **Keihan Line** to **Gion-Shijo Station** or the **Hankyu Kyoto Line** to **Kawaramachi Station**. The area is within walking distance of some of the city's most famous temples, like **Yasaka Shrine** (open 24 hours, free admission) and **Kiyomizu-dera** (open from 6 AM to 6 PM, with an entrance fee of **¥400**). Gion is perfect for those who want to stay in the heart of history while being close to major landmarks. It's a great place to experience **tea houses, traditional shops**, and even book a **geisha performance**. Prices for accommodation here range widely, but if you want to stay in a **traditional ryokan**, it's one of the best areas to do so. Some ryokan in Gion, like **Gion Hatanaka**, offer cultural experiences like **private kaiseki dining** and **tea ceremonies**, though they can be pricey, with stays starting around **¥25,000 per night**.

Arashiyama is a peaceful retreat located on the western edge of the city. It's known for its famous **bamboo groves**, which are a major attraction, but staying here allows you to experience the area early in the morning or later in the evening when the crowds have left. The **Arashiyama Bamboo Grove** is free to visit, and the area is full of **beautiful temples**, like **Tenryu-ji** (open from 8:30 AM to 5:30 PM, with an entrance fee of **¥500**), which is a UNESCO World Heritage site and offers beautiful views of its landscaped gardens. You can also take **boat rides along the Hozu River** or cross the famous **Togetsukyo Bridge**, which offers stunning views of the river and surrounding mountains.

To get to Arashiyama, it's a **15-minute train ride** from **Kyoto Station** on the **JR Sagano Line** to **Saga-Arashiyama Station**. For a more scenic route, you can take the **Hankyu Arashiyama Line** from **Kawaramachi**. If you stay here, the area is dotted with **ryokan** that offer **onsen baths** and traditional meals, like the renowned **Hoshinoya Kyoto**, though be prepared to pay luxury prices starting from **¥50,000 per night**. For something more affordable, you can find smaller inns and guesthouses that offer simpler stays, starting around **¥8,000 to ¥10,000 per night**. Arashiyama is perfect if you want a quiet place to come back to after a day of sightseeing, surrounded by nature.

If **convenience** and **access to everything** are your top priorities, then **Down-**

town is where you'll want to be. This area, around **Shijo Street** and **Karasuma Street**, is a hub of activity with **shopping, dining**, and plenty of transportation options. Staying downtown puts you within walking distance of **Nishiki Market**, known as **Kyoto's Kitchen**, where you can explore food stalls, taste local delicacies, and even find unique souvenirs. Nishiki Market is open from **9 AM to 6 PM**, and while entry is free, bring some cash to try things like **fresh seafood** or **traditional sweets**.

To reach Downtown, you can take the **Karasuma Line** to **Shijo Station** or the **Hankyu Kyoto Line** to **Karasuma Station**. This area is particularly good for **first-time visitors** or anyone looking for quick access to public transport. From here, you can easily catch buses or trains to other parts of the city, like **Kinkaku-ji** or **Fushimi Inari Shrine**. Staying downtown gives you access to a wide range of hotels, from luxury options like **The Ritz-Carlton**, starting at **¥70,000 per night**, to budget hotels like **Daiwa Roynet**, which offers clean, modern rooms starting at around **¥8,000 per night**. You'll also find many mid-range options that offer great value for the convenience of being right in the city center.

When it comes to choosing between a **ryokan** or a **modern hotel**, think about what kind of experience you want. **Ryokan** are a great choice if you're looking for an **immersive Japanese experience**. You'll sleep on **tatami mats**, dine on **kaiseki meals**, and many ryokan offer **onsen baths**—all of which give you a taste of Japanese hospitality and tradition. Staying in a ryokan is perfect if you want to slow down and enjoy a **more serene experience**, particularly in areas like **Gion** or **Arashiyama**. However, ryokan can be expensive, so if you're looking for something more affordable or convenient, modern hotels in **Downtown** or **Gion** are a better fit.

3.2.1 FUSHIMI INARI SHRINE

Fushimi Inari Shrine is a place that stands out with its **thousands of red torii gates**, creating tunnels that stretch up the mountain. These gates are donated by people and companies, and walking through them is an amazing experience. The shrine is dedicated to **Inari**, the Shinto god of rice, business, and prosperity. The shrine itself has been here since **711 AD**, and it's famous for the **fox statues** (called kitsune) that are believed to be Inari's messengers. You'll see these foxes holding keys, symbolizing the protection of rice storehouses, which was a big deal in Japan's history.

The shrine is located in **Fushimi Ward**, south of the city. Getting here is really easy. If you're at **Kyoto Station**, just take the **JR Nara Line** to **Inari Station**—the ride is only about 5 minutes. From the station, it's a **2-minute walk** to the entrance of the shrine. Another option is the **Keihan Main Line** to **Fushimi Inari Station**, which is about 5 minutes walking. The shrine is open **24 hours a day**, and **there's no entrance fee**, so you can go anytime you like.

One of the best things to do here is hike up **Mount Inari**. The **hiking trail** leads through the iconic torii gates and goes up the mountain, reaching about **233 meters** high. If you want to hike to the top, it takes about **2-3 hours round-trip**, but most people stop halfway at the **Yotsutsuji Intersection**, which offers great panoramic views of the city. The higher you go, the fewer people you'll see, making it a more peaceful experience.

If you're into photography or want to avoid crowds, the best times to visit are **early in the morning** or **later in the evening**. If you go around sunrise, the light coming through the trees and gates is stunning, and it's also much quieter. Late evening during sunset is another great time, as the gates seem to glow in the fading light, creating a beautiful atmosphere. Along the way, you'll find **smaller shrines and altars** where people stop to pray or make offerings. You can also buy **fox-shaped ema plaques** to write your wishes on and hang them at the shrine, which makes for a meaningful souvenir. There are also **food stalls** along the trail where you can grab a snack, like grilled mochi or rice cakes, and drinks to keep you going during the hike.

The shrine is especially important during festivals like the **Inari Matsuri**, held every year in February, where people come to pray for good fortune in business and agriculture. The trails through the torii gates and up the mountain, the spiritual atmosphere, and the beauty of the gates themselves make **Fushimi Inari Shrine** a must-see.

3.2.2 KINKAKU-JI (GOLDEN PAVILION)

Kinkaku-ji, also known as the **Golden Pavilion**, is one of the most famous and stunning sights. It was originally built in **1397** as a retirement villa for the **shogun Ashikaga Yoshimitsu**, but after his death, it was turned into a **Zen Buddhist temple**. The pavilion itself is covered in **gold leaf**, and the way it reflects in the **mirror-like pond** in front of it makes the whole scene feel almost unreal. It's a place that perfectly blends nature, architecture, and history.

The pavilion sits in a peaceful garden, and the gold-covered upper floors shine brightly in any season, but how it looks can change dramatically depending on when you visit. In **spring**, the **cherry blossoms** around the temple make it even more beautiful, with pink petals framing the golden building. In **autumn**, the fiery red and orange leaves create a vibrant contrast with the gold, making the scene feel warm and rich. Winter is especially stunning if you're lucky enough to visit after a snowfall—the white snow on the **golden roof** creates a magical, serene atmosphere that's completely unique.

The **grounds of Kinkaku-ji** include not only the pavilion itself but also a **garden** you can walk through. The path takes you around the **pond** and gives you different views of the pavilion, each more breathtaking than the last. You'll also pass by other smaller buildings, statues, and a **tea house**, where you can stop and enjoy some tea while taking in the peaceful surroundings.

The temple is open daily from **9 AM to 5 PM**, and the **admission fee** is **¥400** for adults and **¥300** for children. It's best to visit either **early in the morning** or **later in the afternoon** to avoid the biggest crowds. Since the garden is designed for walking, you can take your time strolling around the pavilion, admiring how the gold leaf shines in different light and reflecting on the calmness of the surroundings. Kinkaku-ji is easy to reach by taking **Bus 101 or 205** from **Kyoto Station**, which takes about **40 minutes,** or you can take a taxi for a quicker but more expensive option. The bus drops you off a short walk away from the entrance. Once inside, you'll follow a **one-way path** around the garden, so navigating is straightforward, and you won't miss any of the key viewpoints. There are also **signs in English** to help guide you through the grounds.

The pavilion's golden exterior and its connection to **Zen Buddhism** make it much more than just a pretty sight.

3.2.3 RYOAN-JI ZEN GARDEN

Daitoku-ji is a quiet temple complex located in the **northern part of the city**, about 15 minutes from **Kyoto Station**. To get there, just take **Bus 205** and get off at **Daitokuji-mae**. It's a short walk from the bus stop, and the whole area feels peaceful compared to the busier temples. You can also take the **Karasuma Subway Line** to **Kitaoji Station** and walk about 15 minutes to reach the entrance. The **bus fare** costs around ¥230, making it an easy trip.

The temple complex is full of smaller sub-temples, each with its own charm. **Zuiho-in** is known for its beautiful **rock garden**, where you can sit and reflect quietly. Another one, **Ryogen-in**, has some of the **oldest Zen gardens** in Japan. These temples are perfect for escaping the crowds and enjoying a peaceful atmosphere. Entrance to the sub-temples usually costs **¥400 to ¥500**, and most are open from **9 AM to 4:30 PM**. Daitoku-ji has a deep connection to **Zen Buddhism**, and it's where the famous **Sen no Rikyū** developed the art of the **tea ceremony**. You won't find tea ceremonies happening every day, but just knowing the history adds to the experience. As you walk around, you'll see small **tea houses** and feel the quiet influence of Zen throughout the gardens and buildings.

If you're hungry after visiting, you can grab a meal nearby. The streets around the temple have small places where you can try local **Kyoto dishes** like **yudofu** (a tofu hot pot) or some **soba noodles**. One good spot for a traditional meal is **Shigetsu**, which serves **shojin ryori** (Zen vegetarian food) in a calm setting, with meals costing around **¥2,000 to ¥3,000**.

You can also visit the small streets around the temple, where you'll find a few **local shops** selling **Kyoto sweets** like **wagashi** or **matcha-flavored treats**. It's a nice way to finish your visit, as these streets are quiet and give you a feel for traditional life in the area. After Daitoku-ji, you can easily walk to **Kinkaku-ji (the Golden Pavilion)**, which is about **15 minutes away**. This makes it easy to see both in one day. **Daitoku-ji** is perfect if you're looking for a more peaceful, less touristy spot to reflect and enjoy the beauty of **Zen gardens**.

3.3.1 GEISHA CULTURE & GION DISTRICT

Gion District is located in the **Higashiyama Ward** in the heart of the city. It's the most famous place to experience **geisha culture**, where you can actually see **geiko** (the local term for geishas) and **maiko** (apprentice geishas) walking through the narrow, atmospheric streets. The district is only a short distance from **Kyoto Station**, and the easiest way to reach it is by taking **Bus 100** or **Bus 206** to the **Gion bus stop**. It's about a **15-minute ride** from the station, and the bus fare is ¥230. You can also use the **Keihan Line** and get off at **Gion-Shijo Station**, which brings you right into the heart of Gion. If you're taking the **Hankyu Line**, **Kawaramachi Station** is also nearby, about a **10-minute walk** away.

The streets of Gion, particularly **Hanami-koji Street** and the **Shirakawa Canal area**, are packed with **wooden machiya houses**, many of which have been standing for centuries. These houses were traditionally used as **teahouses** (ochaya), where **geiko and maiko** perform for guests, entertaining them with dance, music, and refined conversation. As you walk through **Hanami-koji Street**, it's best to go in the early evening when you're most likely to spot a **geiko** or **maiko** walking to their evening engagements. They'll be wearing **elaborate kimonos**, with their faces painted white, and their **obi (sash)** tied in a large bow at the back. Watching them move quietly through the lantern-lit streets is like seeing a moment from the past come to life.

For who is looking to experience the world of **geisha culture** more deeply, you can arrange to attend a **geiko performance**, but this is something that requires special arrangements. Most of the performances happen in **ochaya**, which are not open to the public, so you'll need to book through a high-end **ryokan** or a specialized service. These experiences often include a traditional **kaiseki meal** (a multi-course dinner), with performances of **classical dance** and **shamisen music**, plus a chance to speak with the geiko or maiko about their training and lifestyle. These are premium experiences, and prices typically start at **¥20,000 or more**. It's expensive, but for a real glimpse into this **exclusive world**, it's worth the cost.

Beyond the **geiko and maiko**, Gion itself is a wonderful area to explore on foot. The **Shirakawa Canal**, which runs through part of the district, is lined with **willow trees** and crossed by stone bridges. The reflections of the lanterns on the water make it one of the most picturesque spots, especially at night. The small alleyways off the main streets lead to even quieter corners of the district, where the charm of **old-world Japan** is still very much alive.

When you visit Gion, you can also try some traditional foods. The district has several small restaurants where you can enjoy **kaiseki ryori** (traditional multi-course meals) or lighter options like **soba noodles** and **tempura**. If you want a more casual experience, look for **izakaya** (Japanese pubs) in the area that serve up small plates of **yakitori, sashimi**, and local favorites like **yudofu** (tofu hot pot). Prices vary depending on where you go, but expect to pay around **¥1,500 to ¥3,000** for a casual meal, while high-end dining can easily reach **¥10,000 or more** for kaiseki.

The best way to stay overnight in Giorn is by booking a stay at a **traditional ryokan**. These inns provide not only accommodation but also a **cultural experience**, with rooms featuring tatami mat floors, futon bedding, and traditional baths. Some ryokan can also arrange a **geiko performance** as part of your stay. Prices for a stay in a ryokan in Gion can range from **¥20,000 to ¥50,000** or more, depending on the level of luxury and whether meals are included.

Around Gion, there are many other attractions you can visit. **Yasaka Shrine** is just a short walk from the center of Gion, and it's one of the most important shrines in the city. It's open **24 hours** a day and **free to enter**, making it a great place to visit at night, especially when it's lit up. Nearby, you can also explore the famous **Kiyomizu-dera Temple**, which is about a **20-minute walk** from Gion. It's one of the most visited temples in the city, known for its massive wooden stage that offers panoramic views of the city. Admission to **Kiyomizu-dera** is **¥400**.

3.3.2 PARTICIPATING IN A TEA CEREMONY

Tea houses are often tucked away in **Gion, Higashiyama**, or near **Kiyomizu-dera**, each offering a different setting but always with a strong connection to the past. To reach Gion, you can take **Bus 100** or **Bus 206** from **Kyoto Station** to the **Gion bus stop**, which takes about 15 minutes and costs **¥230**. If you're in the **Kiyomizu-dera** area, you can easily walk to nearby tea houses like **Camellia**.

As you enter the tea house, you'll often walk through a **small garden**, or **roji**, which is meant to transition you from the busy outside world into a more **spiritual, meditative space**. Inside, the **tea room** is usually simple and calming, with tatami mats covering the floor. The door is often low, requiring you to **bow** as you enter—this gesture shows **humility** and sets the tone for the ceremony.

Sitting in the traditional **seiza position** (kneeling) is expected, but don't worry if you aren't used to it—some places allow you to sit cross-legged if needed. The **tea master** performs each step with careful, deliberate movements. The cleaning of the tea utensils is an essential part of the ceremony. It's not rushed because it's about **purity** and **respect**—every step has meaning, even before the tea is prepared.

The host will whisk **matcha** tea in front of you, blending the powdered green tea with hot water into a frothy, rich mixture. When the tea is ready, it's offered to you with both hands. You need to hold the **tea bowl** gently, bow slightly to show **appreciation**, and turn the bowl a little before drinking. This gesture of rotating the bowl is important, showing respect to the host and the bowl itself. Sip the tea slowly, appreciating its bold, slightly bitter flavor. After you finish, wipe the rim of the bowl with your fingers and return it to the host, still holding it with both hands. It's all about **mindfulness** and **being present**.

The tea ceremony is quiet. It's not a time for casual conversation but for reflecting on the moment. You'll likely be offered a **sweet** before the tea, often made from **mochi** or **anko (sweet red bean paste)**. These sweets balance the bitterness of the tea and are an important part of the experience.

Booking a **private tea ceremony** is a great option. Private sessions are more intimate, allowing for closer interaction with the tea master. You'll get a chance to ask questions and better understand the history and importance of each step. Prices for private sessions range from **¥3,000 to ¥10,000**, depending on the tea house and whether you choose a basic or more elaborate experience.

One of the most recommended places for a tea ceremony is **En Tea House** in **Gion**, known for its traditional setup and deep connection to the **geiko** culture nearby. **Camellia Tea House**, close to **Kiyomizu-dera**, is another excellent option, especially for those looking for a more relaxed introduction to the ceremony. Both offer a perfect blend of tradition and accessibility. If you're staying at a **ryokan** in the area, they can often arrange a tea ceremony for you, giving you a fully immersive cultural experience.

When you're finished with the ceremony, take some time to explore what's around you. In **Gion**, you can walk along **Shirakawa Canal**, where **willow trees** drape over the water, offering a peaceful place to reflect on your experience. The area is full of traditional **machiya (wooden townhouses)**, and you might even spot a **geiko** or **maiko** passing by in the evening. If you're near **Kiyomizu-dera**, the temple itself is just a short walk away, offering beautiful views and a chance to visit one of the most famous temples.

If you're hungry afterward, the area around **Gion** has plenty of options for traditional food. You can try a meal at one of the **kaiseki restaurants** for a full multi-course experience, or go for something lighter like **soba** or **tempura** at nearby casual eateries. Expect prices for casual meals to range from **¥1,500 to**

¥3,000, while higher-end meals in **kaiseki** restaurants can go up to **¥10,000 or more**.

3.4.1 NISHIKI MARKET

Nishiki Market is in the middle of the city, running along **Nishikikoji Street**, right next to **Shijo Street**. You can easily get there by taking the **Hankyu Line** to **Karasuma Station** or the **Keihan Line** to **Shijo Station**. Both stations are just a 5-minute walk to the market, and if you're taking the bus, you can hop on **Bus 101** or **Bus 206** and get off at **Shijo-Karasuma**. The market opens around **9 AM** and stays busy until **6 PM**, though it's best to go earlier in the day if you want to avoid the crowds.

The market is famous for being over **400 years old**, and it's packed with more than **100 shops and stalls** offering all kinds of food. You'll find everything here, from **fresh seafood** to **traditional sweets**. As soon as you enter, you'll be surrounded by the smells of **grilled octopus, fresh fish**, and a lot of street food being cooked right in front of you. One thing you have to try is the **grilled squid** or **octopus on a stick**. The seafood here is fresh, and it's usually grilled over open flames, giving it a smoky flavor. You can grab these snacks for around **¥300 to ¥500**, and they're perfect for eating while you walk through the market.

Another must-try is the **taiyaki**, a crispy, fish-shaped pastry filled with **sweet red bean paste** or custard. You'll smell these being made fresh, and they only cost around **¥200 to ¥300**. For something more traditional, try **yatsuhashi**, a soft **mochi** filled with flavors like **matcha** or **cinnamon**. These are local favorites, and you'll find several shops offering free samples so you can taste before you buy.

If you're into **sake**, there are a few stalls where you can do a **sake tasting**. For around **¥500**, you can try different types of local sake, and if you like something, you can buy a bottle to take home. The vendors are helpful and happy to explain the flavors, even if you don't speak the language well.

The market isn't very big, but it's long and narrow, and it can get crowded, especially after lunch. The best way to explore is to move slowly and stop at the stalls that catch your eye. You'll want to try small bites as you go, so don't rush. Most of the vendors are used to tourists and are happy to explain their products. The market is usually busiest in the afternoon, so if you want a more relaxed experience, try to visit earlier in the morning. For a **souvenir**, Nishiki is famous for its **pickles (tsukemono)**. These are made from seasonal vegetables and preserved in all kinds of flavors. They're sold in beautiful packages, and they make a great gift to take home. Prices start at around **¥500**, depending on what you buy. You'll also find some stalls selling **Japanese knives**, which are known for their quality and sharpness. A good knife here can cost around **¥10,000 to ¥20,000**, and some shops will even engrave your name on the blade. After walking around the market, you might want to take a break. There are plenty of **tea shops** nearby where you can sit down and enjoy a cup of **matcha** or a light snack. Some of these places are tucked away in the side streets, so keep an eye out for small signs.

3.5.1 BAMBOO FOREST AT ARASHIYAMA

The **Bamboo Forest at Arashiyama** is one of the most peaceful and iconic places to visit, located in the **Arashiyama District** on the western outskirts of the city. It's incredibly easy to reach, and you can get there by taking the **JR Sagano Line** to **Saga-Arashiyama Station**, which is about a **10-minute walk** from the bamboo grove, or the **Keifuku Line** to **Arashiyama Station**, which is a **5-minute walk** away. If you're coming from **Kyoto Station**, the ride on the **JR line** takes about **15 minutes**, and it's a quick and convenient trip. The forest is open at all hours, and the best time to visit is early in the morning, ideally **before 8 AM**, when it's quiet and less crowded.

The Bamboo Forest itself is located along **Sagano Road**, and as you walk through it, you'll be surrounded by tall, thick bamboo stalks that tower above you, creating a natural canopy. It's an incredibly serene experience—there's a path winding through the bamboo, and as you walk, you can hear the wind rustling softly through the leaves. It's hard not to feel at peace here, and it's the perfect place to **slow down** and take in the moment. The **bamboo pathway** is free to enter, and you can walk through as slowly or as quickly as you want, depending on how much time you have. If you're into photography, the bamboo forest offers some stunning opportunities. The best time for photos is **early**

morning, not just to avoid the crowds but also because the soft light streaming through the bamboo creates a beautiful, ethereal atmosphere. A great tip for photos is to stand at the center of the path, where the bamboo is thickest, and look up—this is where the view feels the most dramatic, with the bamboo stalks reaching up high toward the sky. It's one of the most photographed places in the city.

Close to the bamboo grove is the **Hozu River**, where you can take a **traditional boat ride** for a more peaceful way to see the surrounding area. The boat rides last about **30 to 60 minutes**, depending on the route, and they give you a unique perspective of the beautiful landscape. You'll float past lush green hills, calm waters, and scenic views, making it a perfect complement to your bamboo forest experience. The boat rides typically cost around **¥1,500 to ¥3,000**, depending on the length of the ride and the type of boat you choose.

Once you're done visiting the bamboo forest and the river, there are plenty of other things to do in the area. You can visit the nearby **Tenryu-ji Temple**, one of the most important Zen temples in the city, located just a few minutes from the bamboo forest. This temple is a **UNESCO World Heritage Site**, and its stunning **Zen garden** is a must-see. Admission to **Tenryu-ji** costs ¥500, and it's a peaceful, historical spot that complements the calm atmosphere of the bamboo grove.

For food, there are several local shops and food stalls nearby that offer **yuba (tofu skin)**, which is a local specialty, as well as **green tea-flavored sweets** and **soft-serve ice cream**. These treats are light, refreshing, and perfect for enjoying after a walk through the bamboo forest. You'll also find small restaurants offering **traditional Japanese cuisine**, including **soba** and **tempura**, at reasonable prices, typically around **¥1,000 to ¥1,500** for a casual meal. Theb, I highly recommend heading to the **Hozu River** for a boat ride and then visiting **Tenryu-ji Temple** for a complete day. You have to grab a local snack and take your time, this is a place to **unwind and reflect**, far from the hustle of the city.

CHAPTER 4
OSAKA

4.1 OVERVIEW

4.1.1 STREET FOOD

Dotonbori is located in the busy **Namba** area, and it's one of the best places to experience the street food scene. Getting here is easy—you can take the **Osaka Metro Midosuji Line** to **Namba Station**. It's just a 5-minute walk from there to Dotonbori. If you're coming from **Osaka Station**, the metro ride will take about **15 minutes**. The area is open all day, but it's especially lively at night when the neon lights are bright, and the streets are full of people enjoying the food.

When you arrive, you'll see the famous **Glico Running Man** sign right above the canal. That's how you know you're in the right spot. The streets are lined with food stalls, and the smells of different foods fill the air. One of the must-try items is **takoyaki**, which are small, grilled balls filled with pieces of octopus. You can find them at many stalls, and they cost around **¥500 to ¥600** for a small serving. They're crispy on the outside and soft on the inside, topped with **takoyaki sauce**, **mayonnaise**, and **bonito flakes** that move from the heat. These are made fresh while you wait, so you'll get them hot and ready to eat. Another dish you'll see everywhere is **okonomiyaki**. This is a savory pancake filled with **cabbage**, **pork**, and sometimes seafood. It's grilled on a flat surface, and many places let you cook it yourself at the table. The price for okonomiyaki is usually between **¥700 and ¥1,200**, depending on what you add to it. It's crispy on the outside and soft in the middle, with a rich, savory flavor. It's a lot of fun to cook, and it's a big part of the food culture here.

There's also **kushikatsu**, which are **deep-fried skewers**. You can find all kinds of things on these skewers, like shrimp, pork, vegetables, and even eggs. They're fried until golden and come with a special dipping sauce. Just remember, no double-dipping in the sauce! Each skewer costs about **¥100 to ¥200**, so it's easy to try a variety. Then, take a walk along the **Dotonbori Canal**. The neon lights reflecting off the water create a cool atmosphere, and it's a great place to take photos. If you're still hungry, you'll notice restaurants with huge signs shaped like **crabs** or **blowfish**—those are good spots for seafood lovers.

For a quieter experience, walk over to **Hozenji Yokocho**, a narrow alley with a more traditional feel. You'll find small restaurants serving dishes like **yakitori** (grilled chicken skewers) and places where you can enjoy a drink. The streets are lined with lanterns, and it feels a bit like stepping back in time.

Most of the food stalls and small restaurants only accept **cash**, so make sure you have some with you. Street food prices range from **¥300 to ¥1,200**, so you can eat plenty without spending too much. If you're planning to try a bit of everything, expect to spend about **¥1,500 to ¥2,000**.

4.1.2 HISTORY AND MODERN INFLUENCE

The city is located in the **Kansai region**, easily accessible from most parts of Japan, especially with its connection to the **Shinkansen (bullet train)**, making it a major transportation hub. If you're arriving from **Tokyo**, the train ride to **Shin-Osaka Station** takes around **2.5 hours**, and from **Kyoto**, it's only **15 minutes**. The city is also well-connected through the **Osaka Metro** system, with **Namba Station** and **Umeda Station** being the most popular stops for getting around the city center. These areas are the heart of the city's commerce and entertainment, surrounded by towering **skyscrapers**, luxury shopping streets, and plenty of things to explore.

You'll see how the city's history as a **merchant hub** is deeply woven into its identity. The area near **Shinsaibashi** is one of the best places to feel this mix of old and new. You'll notice traditional **merchant houses**, many of which have been standing for centuries, now transformed into **modern shops** and cafés. This area is famous for high-end shopping, but take your time walking around because it's not just about luxury brands—it's also about experiencing the city's past and how it's embraced change.

If you're curious about the **city's history**, go to the **Osaka Museum of History**, located near **Osaka Castle**. The museum is a great place to dive into the city's role in shaping Japan's economy, starting from its **Edo period** roots as a rice trade center all the way to its role in modern commerce. Admission to the museum is around **¥600**, and it's easily accessible from **Tanimachi 4-chome Station** on the **Tanimachi Line**.

Osaka Castle is one of the city's most iconic spots, a place that symbolizes its history of power and influence. Built in the late 1500s, it played a key role in the **unification of Japan** under **Toyotomi Hideyoshi**. Today, you can visit the **castle grounds**, which are especially stunning during **cherry blossom season**, or go inside the castle to the **museum** for a deeper look at its historical importance. The **castle park** is free to visit, but entrance to the main tower costs **¥600**. It's a short walk from **Osakajokoen Station** on the **JR Osaka Loop Line**.

Around the castle and museum area, you'll find quiet gardens and **green spaces**, offering a peaceful contrast to the bustling streets around **Umeda** and **Namba**. These are the places where you really see how the city manages to blend its **rich history** with modern life. In **Umeda**, the **skyscrapers and high-tech buildings** dominate the skyline, but you'll also find traditional eateries hidden in small alleyways, serving **street food** like **takoyaki** and **okonomiyaki**, which are staples of the city's culinary culture. Takoyaki can be found at various food stalls for around **¥500 to ¥600**, and many places offer their own twist on the traditional recipe.

For off-the-beaten-path, visit **Tenma**. It's a lively district, known for its **old-school atmosphere**, where narrow streets are lined with tiny shops and **izakayas** (Japanese pubs). It's not far from **Tenma Station** on the **JR Loop Line**, and here you'll see a more traditional side of the city. Stop by one of the local bars for some **kushikatsu** (deep-fried skewers) or grab a drink at one of the smaller, hidden bars that often only fit a handful of people. Prices here are incredibly reasonable, with many dishes costing around **¥100 to ¥200 per skewer**, making it a perfect place for a casual meal.

For the **modern architecture**, head to **Umeda Sky Building**, which is not only an architectural marvel but also offers panoramic views of the entire city from its **Floating Garden Observatory**. This building is a prime example of the city's modern edge, with its glass exterior and unique structure, and it's a must-see if you want to appreciate the **cityscape from above**. Tickets to the observation deck are around **¥1,500**, and you can reach it by walking from **Umeda Station**. To getting around, the **Osaka Metro** and **JR lines** are incredibly efficient. The **Osaka Amazing Pass** is a great option if you plan on visiting a lot of attractions, as it offers unlimited rides on public transport as well as free admission or discounts to many of the city's major sights, including **Osaka Castle**, **Umeda Sky Building**, and various museums.

4.2.1 STREET FOOD

As i told you before, **Dotonbori** is located in the **Namba district** at the heart of the city's bustling downtown. To get here, take the **Osaka Metro Midosuji Line** to **Namba Station**, or hop on the **Yotsubashi Line** or **Sennichimae Line**, all of which stop right at **Namba Station**. From there, it's a quick 5-minute walk to reach the lively streets of **Dotonbori**. If you're arriving from **Shin-Osaka Station** via the **JR line**, you can take a direct subway to Namba, which takes about **15 minutes**. The area is accessible day and night, but the best time to visit is in the **evening** when the neon lights light up the streets and reflect off the **Dotonbori Canal**, creating a colorful, electric atmosphere.

Once you're in Dotonbori, you'll know you've arrived when you spot the famous **Glico Running Man** sign towering above the canal. The streets are narrow and packed with food stalls and restaurants, each offering something special. You'll find **takoyaki stalls** on almost every corner—this is the birthplace of the dish, and no trip to Dotonbori is complete without trying these grilled octopus balls. Most stalls sell **takoyaki** for ¥500 to ¥600 for six pieces. You'll see long lines at the best stalls, and waiting in line here is part of the experience, as locals know where the tastiest bites are.

Another highlight is **okonomiyaki**, a savory pancake filled with **cabbage, pork**, or **seafood**, cooked on a flat grill and covered with tangy sauce and mayonnaise. There are many places where you can either have it made for you or cook it yourself at the table. Prices usually range from **¥700 to ¥1,200**, depending on what you choose to add. It's a dish that's both filling and rich in flavor, and you'll find it at stalls along the main street or inside **smaller, family-run restaurants** tucked away in the side alleys.

For something quick and crispy, you'll want to try **kushikatsu**—deep-fried skewers of **meat, vegetables**, and even **cheese**. The skewers are fried to golden perfection and served with a light dipping sauce, which adds just the right amount of flavor. Be sure to follow the local rule: no double-dipping into the communal sauce! Each skewer costs between **¥100 to ¥200**, and you can grab a few while walking around the bustling streets. It's the perfect snack while you explore more of the area. For a break from walking and eating, take a quiet stroll along the **Dotonbori Canal**. You'll find small benches along the water, where you can sit and watch the boats pass by. Around you, the streets come alive, especially at night when the neon lights of the area reflect off the water. This spot offers some of the best views of **Dotonbori's famous signs**, including the **moving crab sign**, which is a local landmark. **Dotonbori** has long been a center of entertainment and food culture, dating back to the **Edo period** when the area was home to kabuki theaters and tea houses. Today, the spirit of entertainment lives on, not just in the food, but in the lively atmosphere that makes one of the most exciting parts of the city to visit.

For visiting something different, visit the nearby streets of **Hozenji Yokocho**, a narrow alley filled with **small izakayas (Japanese pubs)** and **traditional restaurants**. This quieter area is just a 5-minute walk from Dotonbori's bright lights and offers a more relaxed atmosphere. Here, you can sit down and enjoy **yakitori** (grilled chicken skewers) or sip on sake while soaking up the traditional charm. It's also home to **Hozenji Temple**, a small but beautiful temple where visitors splash water on the statue of **Mizukake Fudo** for good luck. And ofcourse, for the evening here, you can easily spend **¥1,500 to ¥2,000** trying different foods and enjoying the atmosphere. The area is open 24/7, but the best time to visit is after dark when the streets are at their liveliest. Keep in mind that many smaller stalls and street vendors only accept **cash**, so it's a good idea to have some yen on hand before you arrive.

4.2.2 KUROMON ICHIBA MARKET

Kuromon Ichiba Market is a famous food market located in the **Nippombashi district**, just a **5-minute walk** from **Nippombashi Station** on the **Sennichimae Line** or **Sakaisuji Line**. It's very close to **Namba** and is easy to reach. If you're coming from **Namba**, it's just a **10-minute walk**. The market is located on **Nipponbashi 2-chome**, and it's packed with more than **150 stalls** offering fresh seafood, local dishes, and ingredients for cooking.

You'll find **sushi and sashimi** stalls everywhere. The fish is incredibly fresh, with options like **fatty tuna**, **salmon**, and **sea urchin**. You can get a small plate of **sashimi** for around ¥500 or enjoy sushi pieces for ¥300 to ¥500 each. The best part is you can eat right at the stall, watching the chefs prepare it. If you're more into grilled seafood, go for the **grilled eel (unagi)**. The sweet soy glaze on top makes it super tasty, and you can get a portion for about ¥1,000. There's also **grilled crab**—a local favorite—sold in portions starting around ¥1,500.

If you're staying somewhere with a kitchen, you can buy fresh fish, **Wagyu beef**, or shellfish to cook yourself. Many stalls will prepare the fish for you, making it easy to take home. **Cooking classes** are also available right at the market, where you can learn how to make sushi or tempura with the ingredients you buy. Classes cost around ¥7,000 to ¥10,000 and take about **two to three hours**.

The market isn't just about seafood ofcourse. You'll also find **fruit stalls** selling super sweet **melons, grapes**, and **strawberries**. Prices for a melon start around ¥1,500, but if you want something cheaper and just as tasty, try **taiyaki**— a fish-shaped cake filled with **red bean paste** or **custard**, costing about ¥300.

The market opens from **9:00 AM to 6:00 PM**, and it's best to visit in the morning when everything is fresh. It gets crowded around lunchtime, so arrive early if you want to avoid the rush. **Bring cash** since many stalls don't take credit cards. The market is fully accessible, with wide walkways for easy navigation. If you're nearby, you can also visit the surrounding area, including **Dotonbori**, which is just a short walk away. You can spend a day enjoying the street food at **Kuromon Ichiba** and then head to **Dotonbori** for the famous neon lights and even more local food.

4.2.3 HIDDEN IZAKAYAS

Hidden izakayas are small, cozy bars tucked away in narrow alleys, perfect for experiencing the local drinking culture. You'll find some of the best ones in **Ura Namba**, a short walk from **Namba Station**. Take the **Midosuji Line** or **Yotsubashi Line** and walk about 10 minutes to the quieter streets. Another great area is **Tenma**, near **JR Tenma Station** on the **JR Loop Line**. Both areas are full of narrow alleys where these hidden bars are located.

Once inside, you'll notice how small these places are—usually seating only about **10 to 15 people**. The vibe is laid-back, with dim lighting and wooden interiors. You can sit at the counter or a small table, depending on the space. People come here to drink **sake** or **shochu** while enjoying small plates of food. Shochu is a stronger spirit, often made from **barley, sweet potatoes**, or **rice**, and you can have it straight, on the rocks, or mixed with water. Sake comes in a variety of flavors—ask the bartender if you want to try something sweet, dry, or fruity.

For food, **yakitori** is a must-try. It's grilled chicken on skewers, and you can choose from different parts like **thighs, wings**, or even more unusual cuts like **hearts** or **livers**. Each skewer costs about ¥150 to ¥200, so you can try several. Another favorite is **karaage**, which is deep-fried chicken—crispy and delicious, usually costing around ¥500 for a small portion. Start with a simple dish like **edamame** (boiled and salted soybeans) to snack on while you sip your drink.

Since most izakayas have menus only in Japanese, it helps to know a few phrases. If you're not sure what to order, just ask **"Osusume wa nan desu ka?"**, which means "What do you recommend?" If the menu has pictures, you can point to something that looks good or see what others are eating.

In **Ura Namba**, you can also visit nearby places like **Dotonbori** for a night out, or if you're in **Tenma**, you're close to **Tenjinbashi-suji**, the longest shopping street in Japan. A night out at an izakaya will typically cost about ¥3,000 to ¥5,000 per person, including drinks and food. These places usually stay open until **midnight** or later, so you can take your time, hopping between bars and trying different dishes. To get there, take the **Midosuji Line** or **Yotsubashi Line** to **Namba**, or the **JR Loop Line** to **Tenma**, and start visiting the small side streets for these hidden gems.

4.3.1 OSAKA CASTLE

Osaka Castle was built by **Toyotomi Hideyoshi** in 1583. It played a huge role in Japan's unification during the feudal period. The original castle was destroyed, but the current one was reconstructed in 1931, standing on the original site. It's located at **1-1 Osakajo, Chuo Ward**, and the best way to get there is by taking the **Osaka Loop Line** to **Osakajokoen Station**, which is a **10-minute walk** from the castle grounds. You can also take the **Tanimachi Line** or **Chuo Line** to **Tanimachi 4-chome Station**, which is about **15 minutes away**.

The **castle grounds** are surrounded by huge moats and stone walls that made it hard to attack in the past. You can walk around the **Nishinomaru Garden,** especially during **cherry blossom season** in late March and early April. The pink flowers cover the trees, and you'll get an amazing view of the castle framed by the blossoms. Entry to the **Nishinomaru Garden** is **¥200,** and it's one of the best places for **hanami** (cherry blossom viewing).

Inside the castle, there's a **museum** where you can learn all about **Toyotomi Hideyoshi** and the **battles that happened here,** especially the **Siege of Osaka** in 1615. You'll see displays of **samurai armor,** weapons, and models of the original castle. Admission to the castle and museum costs **¥600,** and it's open from **9:00 AM to 5:00 PM.** The museum is spread across eight floors, and at the very top is an **observation deck** where you get a **360-degree view of Osaka.** You can see the **city skyline,** the **Osaka River,** and even as far as **Osaka Bay.** It's especially beautiful at sunset, with the light reflecting off the buildings and water.

If you visit during **autumn,** the trees around the castle turn red and orange, making it just as beautiful as the cherry blossoms in spring. It's worth visiting early in the morning to avoid the crowds, especially during peak seasons.

After visiting the castle, you can grab a snack from the street vendors nearby. Popular choices are **takoyaki** (octopus balls) or **yakitori** (grilled chicken skewers), both costing around **¥300 to ¥500.** If you're looking for a bigger meal, head to **Tenmabashi** or **Kyobashi,** both nearby, for **udon, okonomiyaki,** or **sushi.**

You'll need about **2 to 3 hours** to explore the castle grounds, museum, and observation deck. If you want to rent a **bike** and ride around the **Osaka Castle Park,** there are rentals near **Osakajokoen Station** for around **¥500.** The park is huge, and it's a great way to take a breath.

4.3.2 UNIVERSAL STUDIOS JAPAN

Universal Studios Japan (USJ) is located in **Konohana Ward,** Osaka, at **2 Chome-1-33 Sakurajima, Konohana Ward, Osaka 554-0031,** making it easy to access from central Osaka. The best way to reach it is by taking the **JR Yumesaki Line** to **Universal City Station,** just a **5-minute walk** from the park entrance. From **Osaka Station,** the train ride takes about **15 minutes,** and trains run frequently throughout the day. The area around **Universal City** is filled with hotels, shops, and restaurants, so if you're staying nearby, it's a great location to start your day early at the park.

When you enter **USJ,** head straight to **Super Mario World,** the newest and most popular attraction. It's located inside the park, so you'll need to walk a bit, but the excitement starts right when you step through the **Warp Pipe** that takes you into **Mario's world.** The main ride here is **Mario Kart: Koopa's Challenge,** which uses augmented reality to put you in the middle of a race against Bowser. You'll need a **Power-Up Band** to fully enjoy the interactive elements, like hitting virtual blocks and collecting coins. The band costs around ¥3,800, but it's worth it if you want to compete with friends or family.

Another area you should visit is **The Wizarding World of Harry Potter**, home to **Harry Potter and the Forbidden Journey**, a thrilling 4D ride through **Hogwarts Castle**. You can also sip **Butterbeer** at **Three Broomsticks** or shop for magical souvenirs. For **Super Mario World** and **Harry Potter**, the **Express Pass** is a lifesaver. It costs between **¥7,800 and ¥18,800** depending on the season and how many rides you want to skip the line for. The pass is especially useful during **weekends** or **holidays**, when lines can stretch up to **2 hours** for the most popular rides.

If you visit USJ during a **less crowded time**, aim for a **weekday** during **spring** or **autumn**. These are off-peak seasons, and the weather is pleasant for walking around the park. Avoid visiting during **Golden Week** in May or **school holidays** if you want shorter lines. **Summer** can be very hot, and though the park offers **water shows** and cooling stations, it's better to avoid the heat if possible. If you are in the **winter**, you'll get to enjoy the park's **Christmas-themed events**, including the impressive **Christmas tree** and light shows, but it can be cold, so dress accordingly.

Walking around, there are many of **themed restaurants** and snack spots to keep you fueled. In **Super Mario World**, you can dine at **Kinopio's Café** and try **Mario-themed dishes** like **Super Mushroom Pizza** or **Luigi's Green Curry**, with prices ranging from **¥1,500 to ¥2,500**. In the **Wizarding World of Harry Potter**, don't miss the **Butterbeer**—it costs about ¥700 and is a must-try for fans. There are also plenty of **street food** vendors offering quick bites like **popcorn**, **takoyaki**, and **hot dogs**, perfect for grabbing something on the go.

The **park layout** is easy to navigate, with most attractions grouped by theme. You'll want to hit the big rides first—especially **Mario Kart** and **Harry Potter**— before the lines get too long. If you have time, rides like **Hollywood Dream**, **The Amazing Adventures of Spider-Man**, and **Jurassic Park: The Ride** are also popular and offer a mix of thrills and immersive experiences. There's something for every age, from family-friendly attractions to intense roller coasters.

Seasonal events are another highlight at USJ. During **Halloween**, the park transforms into a spooky world with **zombies** and **haunted houses** after dark. In **summer**, you'll find **cool-down events** where water shows keep guests refreshed. And during **Christmas**, the park is decked out in festive lights with **parades** and **holiday-themed shows**. These events bring in larger crowds, but they also add a unique vibe to the park.

Getting back to your hotel or into central Osaka is just as easy as getting to the park. Trains from **Universal City Station** run regularly until **late at night**, so you can enjoy a full day at USJ and still catch a ride back to your hotel. If you're looking for a nearby spot to eat after your day at the park, the **Universal City Walk** area just outside the park is packed with restaurants, serving everything from **Japanese ramen** to **international dishes**.

You should plan to stay at least **8 to 10 hours**, especially if you want to see the parades, try all the rides, and enjoy the food. Ticket prices are around **¥8,400 for adults** and **¥5,400 for children**, but these can fluctuate depending on the season.

4.3.3 UMEDA SKY BUILDING

The **Umeda Sky Building** is located at **1-1-88 Oyodonaka, Kita Ward**, and it's super easy to get there. You can take the **JR Yumesaki Line** to **Osaka Station** and use the **Central North Exit**. From there, it's just a **10-minute walk**. If you're using the subway, get off at **Umeda Station**, and it's about a **10 to 15-minute walk** to the building.

This building has two tall towers connected at the top by the **Floating Garden Observatory**, which gives you an amazing **360-degree view** of the entire city. It's especially beautiful around **sunset**, so aim to be there between **4:30 PM to 5:30 PM** for the best view. You'll see everything from **Osaka Bay** to the distant mountains, and at night, the city lights are incredible.

The **Floating Garden** is open from **9:30 AM to 10:30 PM**, with the last entry at **10:00 PM**, and tickets cost **¥1,500 for adults** and **¥700 for kids**. Once you're up there, you can walk around the observatory and take in the views or relax in the **rooftop garden**. It's a great spot for couples, especially at sunset, but anyone can enjoy the peaceful vibe.

To reach the observatory, you'll take a glass-walled **escalator** between the two towers, which feels like you're floating up into the sky. The building itself was designed by **Hiroshi Hara** and finished in **1993**, and its unique look makes it one of Osaka's most recognizable landmarks.

If you're hungry, head down to the **Takimi Koji** basement level. It's styled like an old **Showa-era street**, with narrow alleys and small, cozy restaurants. You can grab a bowl of **ramen**, some **yakitori**, or try **okonomiyaki**, with prices usually around **¥1,000 to ¥2,000**.

The building is also near other attractions like **Grand Front Osaka** and **HEP Five**, which are great for shopping or even a ride on the **Ferris wheel** if you want more views of the city. But you'll want to spend at least **1 to 2 hours** at the Umeda Sky Building to enjoy the views and maybe grab a bite to eat afterward.

4.4.1 PUBLIC TRANSPORT

To get around the city quickly and easily, you'll mostly rely on the **Osaka Metro system**. It's straightforward and covers all the important parts of the city with **nine lines**, but the most important one you'll probably use is the **Midosuji Line**. It's the main line, running through major districts like **Namba, Shinsaibashi**, and **Umeda**. If you're heading to places like **Osaka Castle**, you'll use the **Chuo Line**, which takes you right to the eastern side. What's really helpful is that all the signs are in English too, so no worries about getting lost.

If you're planning to explore several places in one or two days, the **Osaka Amazing Pass** is worth getting. It gives you **unlimited rides** on the metro and JR lines inside the city, and it includes **free entry** or discounts at over **40 attractions**, including the **Umeda Sky Building, Osaka Castle**, and other cool spots. You can buy it at big stations like **Namba** or **Shin-Osaka**, or even at the airport when you arrive. For one day, it's **¥2,800**, and for two days it's **¥3,600**. This pass will save you a lot, especially if you plan to hit multiple spots.

For JR lines, the **JR Osaka Loop Line** is a super handy route because it circles the city, connecting major areas like **Osaka Station, Tennoji**, and **Tsuruhashi**. If you're heading out of the central part of the city or traveling to nearby places, you'll find this line really useful.

Now, if you're thinking about visiting **Kyoto**, the **JR Special Rapid Service** is the quickest way to get there. It'll take you about **30 minutes** from **Osaka Station**, and the trains are frequent, so you won't have to wait long. You don't need to reserve seats—just hop on and go. For day trips to places like **Nara** or **Kobe**, the JR lines are the best way to get there too, with travel times being around **40 minutes**.

Biking is also a fun option. There are **bike rental stations** all over the city, especially in areas like **Nakanoshima** and along the **Yodogawa River**. If you prefer a more relaxed pace and want to explore quiet neighborhoods, biking is a great way to do it. Some places, like **Namba** or **Shinsaibashi**, are crowded, so be careful biking there, but outside those busy spots, biking offers a flexible and scenic way to see the city.

For convenience, get an **ICOCA card**, which works like a top-up card for the metro, JR lines, and buses. You just tap and go. You can even use it at convenience stores or vending machines, making it much easier than buying single tickets every time.

Public transport here runs from **around 5 AM to midnight**, so it's easy to get where you need to go, whether it's during the day or evening. Everything's clearly marked, so even if it's your first time, you'll quickly get used to the system and move around with no stress.

A. NEIGHBORHOODS TO STAY IN OSAKA

First up is **Namba**. This is right in the heart of the city's action, specifically located along **Dotonbori** and **Shinsaibashi** streets, where you'll be surrounded by some of the best food, entertainment, and nightlife the city has to offer. **Namba** is located in **Chuo Ward**, and the easiest way to get here is by taking the **Midosuji Line** on the **Osaka Metro**. Get off at **Namba Station**, and you're right there—no need for any extra walking. If you prefer the **JR lines**, the **JR Namba Station** is another option. The transport hub here means you can also take a quick train to nearby neighborhoods or even get to **Kansai International Airport** in about **40 minutes** by Nankai Line. When you're in **Namba**, you'll definitely want to try the local street food. Go for the **takoyaki** (fried octopus balls) at any of the stalls along **Dotonbori Street**, which are usually around ¥500-¥700 per serving, or grab some **okonomiyaki**, a savory pancake that's a must-try here. The nightlife in **Namba** is second to none, with endless bars and clubs in the area, particularly around **Hozenji Yokocho**, a narrow street lined with small, traditional bars. It's lively, loud, and fun—perfect if you're someone who thrives on the energy of the city.

For luxury and high-end experiences, you'll want to head over to **Umeda**, located in **Kita Ward**. This is the **business and shopping center** of the city, and you'll find it packed with everything from high-rise department stores to luxury boutiques. To get here, you'll take the **Midosuji Line** to **Umeda Station** or the **JR Osaka Station**. You can also access the area via **Hankyu Umeda Station**, which connects you to other cities like **Kyoto** and **Kobe** easily.

Umeda gives you quick access to some of the best shopping centers in the city, like **Grand Front Osaka**, where you can find international luxury brands, or **Hankyu Department Store**, which has everything from designer clothes to gourmet food floors. **Umeda Sky Building** is another must-see, where you can enjoy a stunning panoramic view of the city for ¥1,500. It's quieter at night compared to **Namba**, but if you're looking for chic rooftop bars or cozy cocktail lounges, this is the area for you. It's perfect for couples or travelers looking for a bit more elegance and comfort in their stay.

Now, for the **traveler who values convenience**, especially if you're planning day trips to other cities, **Shin-Osaka** is your go-to. Located in **Yodogawa Ward**, this area isn't as flashy as **Namba** or **Umeda**, but it's all about the access. **Shin-Osaka Station** is a major hub for the **Shinkansen (bullet trains)**, and from here, you can travel to **Kyoto** in just **15 minutes**, **Nara** in about **45 minutes**, or even take a train to **Tokyo** in **2.5 hours**. To get to **Shin-Osaka**, hop on the **Midosuji Line** and get off at **Shin-Osaka Station**, or take the **JR Line** if you're traveling from other parts of the country. Staying in **Shin-Osaka** is all about **convenience and affordability**. You'll find a lot of business hotels around the station, many of which are well-priced, ranging from **¥6,000 to ¥10,000 per night**, and they're perfect if you're looking for a comfortable but no-frills stay. This area doesn't have the same bustling nightlife or shopping scene as **Namba** or **Umeda**, but it's quiet and practical, especially for travelers who want to get in and out of the city quickly while visiting nearby tourist destinations. You'll find local izakayas and restaurants around the station where you can enjoy a good meal, often at cheaper prices compared to more central districts.

B. ACCOMMODATION OPTIONS FOR EVERY BUDGET

If you want a budget option, **capsule hotels** are the way to go. These tiny pods are super affordable, usually around **¥2,500 to ¥4,500** per night, and they're located in busy areas like **Namba** and **Shinsaibashi**. You'll be right in the middle of things without paying a lot. **First Cabin Namba** is a good pick, just **5 minutes from Namba Station** on the **Midosuji Line**. It's small, but you get clean, simple pods with everything you need. Perfect if you just need a place to sleep and plan to spend your time exploring.

For a bit more comfort, try a **mid-range hotel** or **ryokan**. Prices here are about **¥10,000 to ¥15,000** per night. If you want the real Japanese experience, go for a **ryokan** like **Yamatoya Honten Ryokan** in **Namba**. It's right on **Dotonbori Street**, and you'll sleep on **futons** in a traditional **tatami room**. Some even offer **onsen baths**, which are amazing for relaxing. You'll get traditional service, and they might even serve you a **kaiseki** meal, which is a multi-course Japanese dinner. If you'd rather stay somewhere more modern, **Hotel Monterey Osaka** in **Umeda** offers comfortable rooms with a Western vibe, right near **Umeda Station**.

If you're looking to splurge, the **InterContinental Osaka** in **Umeda** or **Hoshinoya Osaka** in **Shin-Osaka** are top luxury options. Expect to pay **¥35,000 or more** per night. **InterContinental** is close to the fancy **Grand Front Osaka** shopping mall and offers incredible views and service. **Hoshinoya Osaka** is more traditional and feels like a luxury **ryokan**, complete with **onsen baths** and **kaiseki meals**. You'll need to take a **10-minute taxi** from **Shin-Osaka Station** to get there, but it's worth it for the peaceful, riverside experience.

If you prefer staying in a home or apartment, **Airbnb** is another option. You'll find plenty of listings, especially in **Shin-Osaka** or **Nakanoshima**. Just make sure the place has a **Minpaku license**, which means it's legal to rent. Airbnbs are great if you want more space and privacy, especially for longer stays, but be mindful of local rules, like keeping quiet and sorting your trash correctly.

4.5.1 SHINSEKAI DISTRICT

Shinsekai is located in the southern part of Osaka, not too far from **Tennoji**. The easiest way to get there is to take the **Osaka Metro Sakaisuji Line** or the **JR Loop Line** and get off at **Shin-Imamiya Station**. From the station, it's about a **10-minute walk** through narrow streets until you reach the towering figure of **Tsutenkaku Tower**, which is your key landmark for navigating the area. The streets around **Tsutenkaku** are where you'll find the real essence of **Shinsekai**. Built in **1912**, the tower symbolizes the neighborhood's long-standing history. For the best experience, visit the **observation deck** at the top, which is open daily from **9:00 AM to 9:00 PM**, and **tickets cost around ¥800**. From up there, you'll get an incredible panoramic view of the surrounding district and the wider city. Try to go around **sunset** or in the **evening** when the tower lights up—it's a stunning sight that gives the area a cool retro glow.

Now, if you're hungry, **Jan-Jan Yokocho** is the street you need to explore. It's packed with **kushikatsu** restaurants—fried skewers that are a must-try in this part of the city. These deep-fried skewers of meat, vegetables, and seafood range from **¥150 to ¥300** per piece, and you'll see locals lining up at popular spots like **Daruma**, one of the most famous **kushikatsu joints** in the area. Remember the golden rule: **don't double dip your skewer** in the communal sauce! The flavor is rich and satisfying, especially when paired with some **shochu** or local **sake**. If you're exploring in the evening, the area is lively with locals and tourists alike, and it's a perfect place to soak in the street food culture while surrounded by the glowing lights of the area.

For photos, **Tsutenkaku Tower** is your best bet. It's particularly photogenic in the **evening** when the streets and tower light up in a mix of vibrant neon signs. You'll also find vintage arcades nearby, giving you a real sense of the old-world charm that still thrives here. It's gritty, but that's part of **Shinsekai's** allure—you'll get to see a side of the city that hasn't been over-polished by modernity.

In terms of nearby things to do, you're close to **Tennoji Zoo** and **Tennoji Park**, which makes it easy to pair a visit to **Shinsekai** with a more relaxed stop in the park or a trip to the zoo. **Tennoji Station** is just a short walk or metro ride away, connecting you easily to other parts of the city. If you're visiting in the afternoon, this can be a great way to spend the day—hitting **Tennoji** first for some greenery and then finishing off with food and neon vibes in **Shinsekai** by night.

4.5.2 TENNOJI PARK AND HIDDEN TEMPLES

Tennoji Park is a peaceful escape in the middle of the city. It's a quick **5-minute walk from Tennoji Station**, so you can easily get there using the **Osaka Metro Midosuji Line** or the **JR Loop Line**. The park has a lot to offer, and it's great for families or anyone wanting to relax.

If you're with kids or love animals, head to **Tennoji Zoo**. It's been around since **1915**, making it one of the oldest zoos in Japan. Entry is just **¥500 for adults** and **¥200 for children**. You can walk around and see animals like **lions, elephants**, and even **polar bears**. The zoo is open from **9:30 AM to 5:00 PM**, but make sure you enter before **4:00 PM** since that's the last admission time. Mornings are the best time to visit if you want to avoid the crowds.

Not far from the park is the **Shitenno-ji Temple**, which is one of Japan's oldest Buddhist temples, built back in **593 AD**. The temple grounds are free to walk through, but if you want to visit the **inner precinct** or the **treasure house** where the artifacts are kept, there's a small fee, around **¥300 to ¥500**. The temple's **Five-Story Pagoda** is a sight to see, and it's a peaceful place if you want to experience some culture and history.

Inside **Tennoji Park**, you'll also find **Keitakuen Garden**, which is a quiet **stroll garden** with a pond at its center. For just **¥150**, you can walk around and enjoy the views, especially if you visit during **spring** for the flowers or **autumn** for the leaves. The garden is open daily from **9:30 AM to 5:00 PM**, and it's a hidden spot that feels really peaceful.

The **Osaka City Museum of Fine Arts** is also in the park. Tickets are **¥300**, and inside you'll find a collection of **Japanese and Chinese art**, from **scrolls** to **paintings**. The museum is open from **9:30 AM to 5:00 PM**, but it's closed on Mondays. It's small, but worth a quick stop if you're into art.

4.5.3 OSAKA'S SECRET CAT ISLAND

To reach **Ainoshima**, known affectionately as **Cat Island**, you'll first need to make your way to **Shingu Port**. Start by catching a train from **Fukuoka Station** on the **JR Kagoshima Line** to **Shingu Station**, a quick ride of about **15 minutes**. Once you arrive at Shingu Station, it's a short **10-minute walk** to the port, and from there, you'll hop on the **ferry** bound for Ainoshima. The ferry ride itself takes around **20 minutes** and costs roughly **¥500 each way**. It's important to double-check the **ferry schedule** ahead of time because departure times can change depending on the season, but the first ferry typically leaves at **9:00 AM**, and the last one departs the island around **4:30 PM**. Make sure you plan your day accordingly so you don't miss the last ferry back to the mainland.

When you step onto **Ainoshima**, the peaceful atmosphere hits you immediately, as there are no busy streets or major attractions. You'll find yourself surrounded by **cats** from the moment you arrive. They're everywhere—lounging near the **fishing boats**, wandering through the narrow streets, or resting on doorsteps in the **fishing village**. Most of the cats are friendly and used to people, so they won't shy away if you approach them, especially if you bring **cat treats** or some food. The locals, primarily fishermen, care for them, and the cats are a natural part of the island's rhythm of life.

Ainoshima doesn't offer the typical tourist experience—it's not about shops or restaurants. What you'll experience here is a day of **simple, slow-paced life**. You can easily spend hours walking around, taking in the views of the **sea**, visiting the **local shrines**, and watching the fishermen as they go about their daily tasks. While there aren't many dining options, you might find a couple of small eateries where you can taste fresh **grilled fish** or **crab**. The food is basic but fresh, often caught just that morning by the local fishermen. Still, it's best to bring your own **snacks** and **water** to ensure you have everything you need for the day.

Wear **comfortable shoes** because you'll be walking quite a bit—there's no public transport on Ainoshima, and the best way to explore is on foot. The paths are easy to navigate, and you can leisurely wander around the entire island in a few hours. Be sure to take in the **beautiful views of the ocean** and the **simple charm of the fishing village**, where the traditional **Japanese houses** line the narrow streets.

4.6.1 BEST KARAOKE BARS

For trying karaoke in Osaka, head to areas like **Namba**, **Umeda**, or **Shinsaibashi**. These are some of the best places to find karaoke venues. If you're in **Namba**, you can easily reach **Big Echo** on **Dotonbori Street**. Just take the **Midosuji Line** to **Namba Station**, and it's about a **5-minute walk**. Prices during the day are cheaper, starting at **¥300 per hour**, but at night, they can go up to **¥1,000 per hour**.

In **Umeda**, you can visit **Joysound** near the shopping area, a few minutes from **Umeda Station**. You can take the **JR Osaka Loop Line** or the **Midosuji Line** to get there. After singing, you'll have plenty of options for food, like grabbing **takoyaki** or **yakitori** at nearby food stalls.

For karaoke in **Shinsaibashi**, head to **Karaoke-kan** near **Shinsaibashi-suji Shopping Street**. You can take the **Nagahori Tsurumi-ryokuchi Line** or **Yotsub-ashi Line** to **Shinsaibashi Station**. Besides karaoke, this area is great for shopping and seeing the **Glico running man sign** at **Dotonbori**. It's perfect for combining a night of karaoke with a bit of sightseeing.

For local vibe, try **Jankara** or **Shidax**. They're less flashy but great for singing with locals. Booking a room is easy—just walk in, especially during the day. At night, especially on weekends, it's better to call ahead or arrive early. Some places offer **nomihoudai**, which means you can drink as much as you want for an extra **¥1,500 to ¥2,500**. The rooms have song tablets with **English and Japanese songs**, and you can order food and drinks to your room. Most places are open until **5 AM** or even **24 hours**, so you can keep singing late into the night.

4.6.2 OSAKA'S PARTY SCENE

Take the **Midosuji Line** straight to **Namba Station**. From there, walk to **Doton-bori**, the busiest nightlife area in the city. The neon signs and packed streets will lead you to **Giraffe**, one of the biggest clubs. It's got different floors with different kinds of music—whether you like hip-hop, pop, or electronic beats, you'll find something to dance to. If you get there before **11 PM**, you might save some money since entry is about **¥2,500**, but early birds or on ladies' nights, there are usually discounts. Drinks inside will cost you around **¥800**, but you can always grab some street food before entering, like **takoyaki** or **okonomiyaki** from nearby food stalls, especially around the canal.

For a relaxed night, hop on the **JR Osaka Loop Line** and head over to **Umeda Station**. This is where you'll find **Mister Kelly's Jazz Club** on **Doyama-cho Street**, a cozy spot for live jazz performances. It's a smaller venue, so it feels inti-mate, and the music is great if you want to chill with a drink. Expect to pay **¥1,500** for entry and around **¥1,000 to ¥1,500** for drinks, but it's worth it for the laid-back atmosphere. While you're in **Umeda**, there's also **Bar Augusta**, a whiskey bar that's a must-visit if you're into Japanese whiskeys like **Yamazaki** and **Hibiki**. Drinks here range from **¥1,200 to ¥2,500**, depending on what you order, and it's a nice quiet spot for a slower night.

For a local vibe, both **Namba** and **Umeda** have tiny hidden bars tucked away in backstreets. In **Namba**, check around **Amerika-mura** or near **Shinsaibashi** for hole-in-the-wall bars where most of the patrons are locals. Many of these places don't have big signs outside, but that's part of the charm. The same goes for **Umeda**—if you wander off the main roads near **Grand Front Osaka**, you'll discover small whiskey bars or **izakayas** that offer a more authentic, laid-back experience. Even if the menu is only in Japanese, you can point at drinks or ask for a recommendation, and you'll be set.

The last trains, like those on the **Midosuji Line** and the **JR Osaka Loop Line,** stop around **midnight,** so if you're planning to stay out late, you might need to find other options for getting back to your hotel. But no worries, if you miss the last train, karaoke places or **24-hour izakayas** are good ways to wait until the first trains start running again at **5 AM**. Karaoke is big in Japan, and these spots are all over, especially near the train stations. You'll pay about **¥1,500** for a few hours, and some places offer **nomihoudai** (all-you-can-drink) deals. It's a fun way to spend the late hours with friends if you're looking to keep the night going.

CHAPTER 5
HOKKAIDO

5.1 OVERVIEW

5.1.1 THE GREAT OUTDOORS OF JAPAN'S NORTHERN FRONTIER

Hokkaido is Japan's northern wilderness, full of beautiful mountains, forests, and clear lakes. It's a place where you can experience the outdoors in both summer and winter, and it's very different from the rest of Japan. You can get there by flying into **New Chitose Airport**, just outside **Sapporo**, or by taking a **JR train** from other parts of Japan. If you plan to visit the more remote spots, renting a car is a good idea since the train lines don't reach everywhere.

In the summer, the weather is perfect for **hiking and walking through flower fields**. You'll want to visit **Furano** for its lavender fields, which are at their best in **July**. You can get there by taking the **JR Furano Line** from **Asahikawa**. The fields are perfect for photos, and nearby farms serve delicious **ice cream** made from Hokkaido's famous **dairy**. You'll find food stalls and small cafes where you can grab a bite to eat for around **500 to 1500 yen**. If you like fresh farm produce, it's a great place to try some **local cheese** and **dairy products**.

If you prefer the **snow**, **Niseko** is the place to go for skiing. It's easy to reach by train, just take the **JR Hakodate Line** from Sapporo. Niseko is famous for its

soft powder snow, and if you ski or snowboard, it's one of the best places in Japan. You can rent gear for around **4000-7000 yen per day**, and there are plenty of **onsen** (hot springs) nearby where you can relax after a long day on the slopes. The view from the hot springs is stunning, especially in the winter.

Another spot for nature lovers is the **Shiretoko Peninsula**, which is a **UNESCO World Heritage Site**. You can take a train to **Shari Station** and then a bus to **Utoro Port**. From there, you can take a **boat tour** to see **brown bears** and **rare wildlife** along the rugged coastline. These tours cost around **5000-8000 yen** but are worth it if you love nature. You can also take **guided hikes** along the coast, but it's best to go with a guide to stay safe since the area is very wild.

For a calmer experience, visit the **Blue Pond** in **Biei**, a short bus ride from **Asahikawa Station**. The pond is known for its bright **blue color**, which changes depending on the season and weather. It's a perfect spot for photography, especially early in the morning when the light hits the water just right. There are walking trails nearby if you want to explore more of the natural surroundings, and it's free to visit.

In winter, **Hokkaido** transforms into a **snowy wonderland**, with thick snow covering everything, making it perfect for skiing, snowboarding, and enjoying hot springs in a serene setting.

5.1.2 ESSENTIAL GEAR FOR EVERY SEASON

When you're heading to Hokkaido, what you pack depends a lot on the season and the activities you've got planned. In winter, if you're going skiing at places like **Niseko** or **Furano**, you'll definitely need **thermal layers** to keep you warm, a **waterproof jacket**, and solid **snow boots** that can handle walking through deep snow. **Insulated gloves** are essential because it gets freezing, especially if you're skiing or snowboarding all day. Most people rent their ski gear on-site, and you can expect to pay about **¥10,000-¥15,000** a day for rentals, including skis, boots, and poles. To get to these resorts, take the **JR Hokkaido Rail** to **Kutchan** (for Niseko) or **Furano**—it's super easy to catch a train from Sapporo and transfer to a shuttle bus at the station.

In summer, Hokkaido's trails and parks are perfect for hiking, so you'll want **light hiking boots** that give you good grip and breathable layers to stay comfortable. The weather can change fast in the mountains, so pack a **light jacket** or **windbreaker** in your backpack. If you're exploring **Daisetsuzan National Park**, you can take a train to **Asahikawa** and then a **bus** to the park entrance, which takes about **60 minutes**. Get there early—buses tend to get crowded around **7 a.m.**, especially during peak hiking season. And if you're into photography, bring an extra camera battery because the views are stunning, and you'll want to take lots of photos, especially around sunrise or sunset.

For **onsen (hot springs)**, like the remote onsens in **Jozankei** (which is a short **40-minute bus ride** from Sapporo), you'll need to pack differently. Bring a **small towel** (onsen hotels sometimes provide these), a **change of clothes**, and slippers for walking around the hot spring areas. Onsen etiquette is really important here —make sure to **wash thoroughly** before getting into the baths, and keep quiet because it's a relaxing place. In the winter, places like the **Blue Pond in Biei** are magical with snow covering the ground, but it's cold, so make sure your camera is protected, and pack extra batteries. The best time for photos is usually early in the morning or just before sunset.

5.2.1 DAISETSUZAN NATIONAL PARK

Planning a trip to **Daisetsuzan National Park**, the first thing you need to know is how vast and diverse this area is. Located in the **center of Hokkaido**, this park spans over **2,267 square kilometers** and is home to some of the wildest and most beautiful landscapes in all of Japan. You'll be heading towards the towns of **Asahidake Onsen**, **Sounkyo Gorge**, or **Furano** depending on which part of the park you want to explore.

If you're starting in **Asahidake**, the easiest way to get there is to take a train to **Asahikawa Station** and from there, catch a bus (about a 1-hour ride) to **Asahidake Onsen**. Buses run **several times a day** and cost around **¥1,400** one-way. If you're traveling by car, there's a **parking lot** at the base of **Asahidake Ropeway** where you can leave your vehicle before taking the cable car up into the mountains.

The **Asahidake Ropeway** is open year-round, with the first cable car going up at **6:30 AM in the summer** and around **8:30 AM in the winter**. Tickets for the **ropeway** cost **¥2,200 for a round trip**, and it's a convenient way to access some of the park's best hiking trails without needing to do a full summit hike. Whether you're a casual hiker or looking for more intense treks, Asahidake is the perfect starting point.

Another popular entry point to **Daisetsuzan** is **Sounkyo Gorge**, famous for its waterfalls and stunning autumn colors. You can get there by taking a bus from **Kamikawa Station**, a 30-minute ride that'll set you back about **¥870**. Sounkyo is more developed than other parts of the park, with several onsen resorts, restaurants, and hotels. **Ryokan** stays here can cost anywhere from **¥12,000 to ¥25,000 per night**, with meals included. Don't miss a visit to **Ryusei and Ginga Falls**, just a short walk from the town center.

For a more rugged experience, **camping in Daisetsuzan** is a fantastic option. You'll find **campgrounds** in the **Asahidake Onsen** and **Sounkyo** areas, and you can set up your tent for around **¥500 to ¥1,000 per night**. Basic facilities like restrooms are available, but you'll need to bring your own gear and food. For something more adventurous, head towards **Mt. Tomuraushi** for a **two-day camping hike**, where you'll sleep under the stars surrounded by pristine nature. Be prepared for **no facilities** here—it's a true wilderness experience.

Hiking is the main attraction in Daisetsuzan, and the trails range from easy to challenging. If you're new to hiking, try the **Asahidake Sugatami Pond Trail**, a **45-minute loop** around a beautiful volcanic pond that offers amazing views of the surrounding mountains. More experienced hikers can take on the **Asahidake Summit Trail**, which takes about **4-6 hours round trip**. Don't forget your **layers and windproof clothing**—even in the summer, it gets cold as you ascend, and the weather can change fast.

If you are hungry, i suggest you to try the traditional **kaiseki meals** served at **ryokan** in **Asahidake Onsen** feature seasonal ingredients from the region. For something more casual, try **Sounkyo Onsen**'s local eateries serving up **Hokkaido's famous miso ramen** for about **¥900 per bowl**, or head to one of the small restaurants near **Asahidake Onsen** for fresh **soba noodles** and **tempura**.

Daisetsuzan, in the summer, you'll find **wildflower meadows** in full bloom, while the fall offers some of the most stunning **autumn foliage** in Japan. If you're visiting in winter, the park becomes a **snow-covered wonderland**, perfect for **snowshoeing** or skiing in the nearby resorts of **Furano** and **Asahidake**.

Asahikawa, the nearest city, is also a great place to stock up on supplies or enjoy a meal before heading into the wilderness, and you can also visit the **Asahiyama Zoo** if you have time.

5.2.2 SAPPORO SNOW FESTIVAL

The **Sapporo Snow Festival** takes place in three main locations throughout **Sapporo City**, each offering a unique experience. The most famous spot is **Odori Park**, which stretches over 1.5 kilometers in the center of the city along **Odori Street**. To get there, take the **Sapporo Subway's Namboku Line** to Odori **Station**, which is just a 2-minute walk from the park. You'll find **giant snow sculptures** here, some as tall as buildings, alongside smaller but incredibly detailed creations. The park is lined with food stalls selling local Hokkaido treats like **grilled squid, corn**, and **hot bowls of ramen** to warm you up as you visit.

At night, the snow sculptures are illuminated, creating an almost magical atmosphere. Visiting between **4:30 PM and 10 PM** is ideal for enjoying the **light displays**, especially as the crowds thin out in the evening. The best spots for photos are near the **Sapporo TV Tower**, located at the east end of Odori Park, where you can capture stunning views of the sculptures with the tower in the background. Entry to the festival is free, but keep in mind that food stalls and nearby restaurants are typically a bit pricier during the festival, with dishes like **grilled seafood** or **Hokkaido's famous crab soup** costing around **500 to 1,500 yen.**

The second major site is **Susukino**, located about **15 minutes away** from **Odori Park** by walking, or a quick one-stop ride on the **Namboku Line** to **Susukino Station**. This area is famous for its **ice sculptures** that reflect the lights of the vibrant nightlife district. At Susukino, the sculptures are often intricate and lifelike, featuring animals, famous landmarks, and artistic designs. The **Susukino Ice World** event runs alongside the festival, making it a must-visit after you've explored the snow sculptures at Odori. Because the area is packed with locals and tourists alike, it's best to visit between **7 PM and 9 PM** to fully appreciate the illuminated sculptures before the crowds grow. Susukino is also known for its bustling izakayas and ramen shops—perfect for a late-night bite after the festival.

For families, the **Tsudome Site** offers a more hands-on, interactive experience. This is located about **30 minutes** from central Sapporo, and you can catch a **shuttle bus** from **Sakaemachi Station** (on the **Toho Subway Line**). Here, the vibe is more relaxed and playful, with activities like **snow slides**, **snow rafting**, and even a snowball fight area. The **snow domes** are particularly fun, as you can enter and experience what it's like inside a cozy snow hut. This is a great spot for kids, and even if you're an adult, you'll find plenty of reasons to enjoy. A shuttle bus from **Odori** or **Sapporo Station** is the easiest way to get there, with buses running every **20–30 minutes** during the festival. The shuttle fare is around **100 yen**, and entry to Tsudome is free.

Each site offers plenty of **food options**, at Tsudome, look for stalls selling **hot Hokkaido corn, potato croquettes**, and even **soup curry**—a local specialty. Prices for food range from **300 to 1,500 yen** per dish, depending on what you choose, and many of the food stalls accept both cash and card.

While the **Sapporo Snow Festival** officially runs for about **a week in early February**, specific dates vary each year, so it's best to check the official festival website closer to your visit. For the best experience, try to visit during the weekdays, when it's less crowded, and make sure to dress warmly, as temperatures often drop to **-10°C or lower**. Bringing **thermal layers, snow boots, gloves**, and a **hat** is essential, along with a **weatherproof camera bag** if you plan to take lots of pictures.

5.2.3 SKIING AND SNOWBOARDING

Niseko is located on **Japan's northern island of Hokkaido**, about **100 kilometers west** of **Sapporo**, and is part of the **Mount Annupuri range**. To get there, you'll likely fly into **New Chitose Airport**, which is the main airport serving **Sapporo**. From the airport, there are multiple ways to reach Niseko. The easiest option is the **direct shuttle buses** that operate regularly, taking around **2–2.5 hours** to get you straight to your accommodation. Buses depart frequently, and you can catch one near the domestic or international terminals at the airport. If you prefer trains, you can take the **JR train** to **Otaru Station** and then transfer to the **Hakodate Line** for a train ride to **Kutchan Station**, where most Niseko visitors get off. From there, you'll find hotel shuttles or taxis ready to take you to your final destination in Niseko.

Once you're there, **Niseko's main village area—Hirafu**—is the heart of the action, where you'll find everything from **boutique hotels** to **traditional ryokan**, as well as plenty of bars and restaurants to explore after a long day on the slopes. **Hirafu's streets**, like **Hirafu-zaka Street**, are packed with shops selling ski gear, souvenirs, and some of the best eateries around. You'll want to try **Niseko's famous Hokkaido dairy-based dishes** like creamy hot **ramen** or the melt-in-your-mouth **cheese tarts** that you can grab from local bakeries like **Milk Kobo**. If you're up for a splurge, try **Niseko's famous seafood**, such as **uni (sea urchin)** or **crab dishes**, which are a must after hitting the cold slopes.

For skiing, **Niseko United** is the resort to go to, and it connects **four ski areas**: **Grand Hirafu, Hanazono, Niseko Village**, and **Annupuri**. A **full-day pass** typically costs around **7,500 yen**, though you can save by booking multiple-day passes in advance. You can rent your ski or snowboard equipment from any of the rental shops in **Hirafu** or **Niseko Village**, where prices range from **4,000–6,000 yen** depending on the type of gear you need. The runs are open from **8:30 AM to 4:30 PM** for most areas, with some night skiing options that run until **8:30 PM**, which is perfect if you want to avoid the daytime crowds and ski under the stars.

For a off-the-beaten-path skiing, **Furano** offers an equally stunning option but with fewer crowds. Located about **120 kilometers northeast of Sapporo**, you can take a **train** from Sapporo on the **Furano Line** or a direct bus from **Asahikawa Airport**, which is a faster route. Furano is famous for its soft powder and quiet slopes, making it ideal for a relaxed trip. The resort area is a bit more spread out, and the town itself has a slower, more local vibe compared to Niseko's international flair. You can explore **Furano's backcountry** for some real adventure, or stick to the groomed runs that cater to all skill levels. A day pass here is slightly cheaper than Niseko, costing about **5,500 yen**. The best times to visit either **Niseko** or **Furano** are from **late December to early March**, when the snow is at its best.

In Niseko, after a day on the slopes, nothing beats relaxing at one of the area's famous **onsen (hot springs)**. Many of the **ryokan** and resorts have their own **onsen** facilities, and some are open to the public for around **700–1,200 yen** per visit. One highly recommended onsen is **Yukoro Onsen** in **Hirafu**, where you can soak while overlooking snowy landscapes—perfect for winding down. Make sure to follow traditional onsen etiquette: wash thoroughly before entering the baths, and note that tattoos may need to be covered in some places.

For a quieter night and want to visit a more local vibe, **Furano** also has plenty of smaller **izakayas** (Japanese-style pubs) where you can try local specialties like **Hokkaido lamb**, often cooked **jingisukan-style** (a grill right at your table). Try the local **sake**, which is perfect after a long day in the cold.

5.3.1 SHIRETOKO PENINSULA

To get to **Shiretoko Peninsula**, one of the most remote and wild places in Japan, start by heading to **Shari Town in Hokkaido**. You can take a **JR Limited Express train** from Sapporo to **Shari Station**, which takes about **6 hours**, and then hop on a **bus to Utoro**, the main gateway to the peninsula. The bus runs several times a day, and the ride costs around **1,500-2,000 yen**. Once you arrive in Utoro, you're ready to visit.

Shiretoko is all about raw, untouched nature, and it's one of the best places in Japan for wildlife spotting and hiking. The **Shiretoko National Park** is where you'll want to start. The **Shiretoko Five Lakes** are a must-see, especially if you love hiking. The trail around the lakes is easy and offers some of the best views of the **Shiretoko mountain range** reflecting in the water. The trail opens from **late May to early October**, and it's especially beautiful in the summer when the wildflowers bloom. Be aware that if you visit between **May 10 and July 31**, you'll need a guided tour because of bear activity in the area.

You can join a **bear-watching cruise** from **Utoro Port**. The cruises last around **1.5 to 2 hours** and cost **5,000 yen** per person. These cruises take you along the coastline, where you'll likely spot **Ezo brown bears** and enjoy incredible views of the cliffs and forests that make Shiretoko so special.

If you're into something less intense, head to **Furepe Falls**, known for its gentle cascade into the sea. It's just a short **20-minute walk** from the visitor center, and it's especially stunning during sunset. The best part is it's an easy walk, making it perfect for families or those looking for a more relaxing experience.

During winter, from **February to March**, the sea around Shiretoko freezes over with **drift ice**, creating a magical white landscape. You can take a **drift ice cruise** from **Rausu**, a small town about 45 minutes from Utoro. These cruises cost around **3,000 yen** and offer the chance to see **Steller's sea eagles** and other wildlife.

Shiretoko also has some hidden gems, like **Kamuiwakka Hot Falls**, a natural hot spring waterfall. You can soak in the warm water after a hike, but you'll need to rent a car to reach it since there's no public transport. It's free to visit, and the warm water cascading down the rocks is a one-of-a-kind experience. For food, Utoro has great seafood options. Check out **Shiretoko Dining** on **Utoro Nishi-machi Street** for fresh **uni (sea urchin)**, **crab**, and **salmon roe**. Meals range from **1,500-4,000 yen**, and the seafood is straight from the nearby waters.

5.3.2 THE BLUE POND IN BIEI

The **Blue Pond**, known locally as **Aoiike**, is located in the **Shirogane area** of **Biei**, a small town in **Hokkaido's Kamikawa District**. This quiet, picturesque pond sits about **17 kilometers** east of **Biei Station**, which makes it an easy day trip if you're in the area. To reach the pond, you can take the **Furano Line train** from **Asahikawa Station** to **Biei Station**, and from there, you can either catch the **seasonal bus** heading to the **Shirogane Hot Springs** area or rent a car if you prefer more flexibility with your travel times. The bus journey takes about **30 minutes** and costs around **500 yen** one way.

For public transport, the bus stop near **Biei Station** is conveniently located, but be aware that services can be less frequent in the off-season, so plan accordingly. If you're visiting in **summer** or **autumn**, the buses run more regularly, making it simple to explore without a car. If you choose to drive, there is **free parking** available near the pond, but keep in mind that winter roads in Hokkaido can be icy, so driving experience in snowy conditions is recommended if you're coming during the colder months.

Once you arrive, you'll find that the **Blue Pond** is free to visit, and it's open all day, making it a perfect stop whether you're an early riser or looking to visit in the afternoon. The area around the pond is quite peaceful, and the walking trails allow you to take your time, capturing photos from different angles. If you're wondering when the best time to visit is, **early morning** or **late afternoon** offers the most beautiful lighting and reflection on the water's surface. The vibrant blue color of the pond can change depending on the season and the time of day, making every visit a little different.

The pond itself is part of a larger natural area that includes the nearby **Shirogane Onsen**, a small hot spring village known for its relaxing outdoor baths surrounded by nature. After spending time walking around the pond, you can head to the hot springs for a soak—perfect for easing tired muscles after a day of exploring. Entry to the onsen typically costs around **700–1,200 yen** depending on the facility, and it's well worth it if you want to experience Hokkaido's famous onsens.

When you're in the area, don't miss out on **Biei's local eateries**. The town is known for its fresh produce and dairy, so you can find delicious **soft cream (soft-serve ice cream)** made from Hokkaido's famous milk at many of the cafes. If you're hungry after your visit to the pond, stop by one of the small restaurants near **Biei Station** that serve hearty meals like **Biei curry rice** or **ramen**. Prices for food range from **800 to 1,200 yen** depending on what you choose.

5.3.3 HIDDEN ONSEN IN NATURE

Nyuto Onsen is hidden in the mountains of Hokkaido, a really peaceful place where you can enjoy hot springs surrounded by nature. It's part of the **Akan Mashu National Park**, and you'll find the onsen tucked away in a quiet area that feels like stepping back in time. To get there, you'll take the **JR Akita Shinkansen** to **Tazawako Station**, which is about a 3-hour trip from **Tokyo**. Once you reach Tazawako Station, hop on the **Ugo Kotsu Bus** that goes to **Nyuto Onsenkyo**, and it'll take about **45 minutes** to get to the hot springs. The bus ride costs around **1,200 yen** one way.

The most popular onsen is **Tsurunoyu Onsen**, one of the oldest in the area, dating back to the **1600s**. The outdoor baths, known as **rotenburo**, are surrounded by mountains, and the water here is milky white because it's full of minerals like sulfur, which are believed to be great for your skin. The entrance fee is about **600 to 1,000 yen** depending on where you go, but if you're staying overnight, rooms can range from **10,000 yen per person**, including meals. **Magoroku Onsen** is another good option if you want something a little quieter, with fewer visitors.

For a meal, the local specialty is **kiritanpo nabe**, a hotpot with grilled rice sticks and chicken, perfect for warming up after a long day in the hot springs. Meals typically cost between **800 yen to 2,000 yen** at nearby restaurants or the ryokan where you're staying.

Nearby, you can visit **Lake Tazawa**, which is the deepest lake in Japan and only **20 minutes** by car from the onsen. It's beautiful for a quick stop, especially in the evening when the light reflects on the water. You can also hike **Mount Akita-Komagatake**, which is about a **5-6 hour** trek for those looking for more adventure.

Winter, i think is the best time to visit Nyuto Onsen, from **December to March**, when everything is covered in snow, making it feel like a winter wonderland. If you prefer **autumn**, the changing colors of the leaves around the onsen are breathtaking. Even in summer, it stays cooler than other parts of Japan, so it's a great escape from the heat.

Bring a **towel**, as some places may charge extra for one, and if you're visiting in winter, make sure to pack warm, waterproof shoes for walking around the snow-covered paths.

5.4.1 SAPPORO'S FAMOUS RAMEN

Heading to **Ramen Alley** in **Sapporo**, you'll find it right in the busy **Susukino** district, one of the city's best spots for food and nightlife. It's really easy to get there—just take the **Namboku subway line** and hop off at **Susukino Station**. The alley is just a 5-minute walk away. If you're coming from **Sapporo Station**, it's only a quick 5-minute subway ride. Ramen Alley is located on **Minami 5 Jonishi 3-chome**, and you can spot it easily because it's a small street full of ramen shops.

The ramen here is famous for a reason. This is where you'll find the classic **Sapporo miso ramen**. The broth is rich, savory, and full of flavor, often topped with butter and corn, which is a local favorite. One of the best places to try it is **Shirakaba Sansou**. A bowl of their ramen will cost you around **800 to 1,200 yen**, depending on what you order. You can also check out **Aji no Karyu**, another popular spot that's been serving ramen for decades. If you're up for something different, try their **crab ramen** for a true taste of Hokkaido.

Ramen Alley is perfect for a late-night bite since most of the shops stay open until **1:00 AM**, but it's better to go early because the lines can get long, especially at the most famous places. The alley is even more fun to visit in the winter when the snow falls, and the city lights up. It's cozy and exciting at the same time.

If you want a quieter ramen experience, you can walk about **15 minutes** to the area around **Odori Park**, where there are more ramen shops without the big crowds. It's a great option if you want something a little less hectic but still delicious.

After eating, you can explore **Susukino**'s nightlife. The area is full of bars, pubs, and shops like **Tanukikoji Shopping Street**, where you can find local souvenirs and snacks.

Getting there is easy, with trains on the **Namboku Line** running until around **11:30 PM**, and there are buses too. If you're driving, keep in mind that parking around Susukino can be expensive, so it's better to stick to public transport.

5.4.2 HOKKAIDO DAIRY AND CHEESE

Hokkaido's lush farmlands produce top-quality milk, cheese, and ice cream, and there are several spots you absolutely can't miss.

Milk Kobo near **Niseko** is a must-visit. This place is a **15-minute drive from**

Niseko Station, or you can take the hourly bus service that drops you just a short walk away. The farm's dairy shop is open from **10:00 AM to 6:00 PM**, and the famous soft cream, priced at **350-400 yen**, is made fresh with Hokkaido milk. You can also sign up for their **ice cream-making classes** that usually cost around **2000 yen**. For parking, there's ample space, so renting a car is convenient if you prefer driving. Nearby, you'll find **local eateries** offering Niseko's fresh produce and delicious dairy-inspired menus.

In **Furano**, head to the **Furano Cheese Factory**, located just **20 minutes from JR Furano Station** by bus. The buses run frequently, but if you prefer to drive, there's a **parking lot** available right at the factory. Their **cheese-making workshops** are popular and fill up quickly, so it's best to reserve your spot in advance online or through your hotel concierge. These workshops cost about **1000-1500 yen** per person, and you'll also get to taste their signature black cheese made with bamboo charcoal. The factory is open from **9:00 AM to 5:00 PM**, and after the workshop, you can explore the peaceful **Furano countryside** or visit nearby **Furano Winery** to pair local wines with the cheese you've just made.

If you're in **Sapporo**, make sure to visit **Shiroi Koibito Park**, which is easily accessible via **Miyanosawa Station** on the Tozai subway line. It's a 10-minute walk from the station, and you can also take local buses from downtown Sapporo that stop nearby. This park offers a sweet mix of factory tours where you can see how their famous chocolates and soft cream are made. Entry is free for the **garden area**, but if you want to join the factory tour and create your own chocolate, prices start at around **800 yen**. The **soft cream**, a highlight, costs around **400 yen** and is served at their café overlooking a beautiful garden. The park operates daily from **9:00 AM to 6:00 PM**, and it's a good idea to arrive early to avoid long lines, especially during peak tourist seasons.

In **Hakodate**, the **Hakodate Morning Market** is located directly outside **JR Hakodate Station**. It's open from **6:00 AM to noon**, and although it's mostly famous for seafood, you'll also find stalls selling freshly churned soft cream for **300-400 yen**. The market is a great place to stroll around after grabbing breakfast or exploring the nearby **Motomachi district**, where you can admire the city's **historic Western-style buildings**.

5.4.3 HOKKAIDO SEAFOOD SPECIALTIES

Hakodate Morning Market is the perfect place for fresh seafood. It's a short 5-minute walk from JR Hakodate Station on Wakamatsu-cho Street, and it opens early, around 5:00 or 6:00 AM, and closes by noon. You'll find rows of stalls selling live king crab, oysters, sashimi bowls, and other seafood. The market is known for its **uni-don**, which is a rice bowl topped with sea urchin, and usually costs between **2000 to 3000 yen**. If you love seafood, this is a great place to try it. If you want something grilled, look for vendors grilling crab legs or scallops. These cost about **1000 yen per piece**, and they are cooked right in front of you, making it a real treat.

If you're in Sapporo, visit **Nijo Market**, just a 10-minute walk from **Odori Station**. It opens around **7:00 AM** and is great for seafood, especially kaisen-don, which is a sashimi rice bowl, typically priced between **1500 and 3500 yen**. The market is lively in the mornings, and many stalls have seafood displayed in tanks or on ice. It's also an ideal place to pick up seafood to take home, and they offer shipping services for fresh crabs. Don't miss trying grilled squid or scallops here for around **500 to 800 yen**.

If you're near **Otaru**, go to **Otaru Sankaku Market**, which is right next to JR **Otaru Station**. The market is smaller but known for its **ikura-don**, a salmon roe rice bowl that costs around **2500 yen**. Otaru itself is a scenic town, and after you've had your seafood fix, explore the nearby shops selling glassware and music boxes.

All of these markets open early, so it's best to go between **6:00 and 8:00 AM** for the freshest seafood. **Hakodate Morning Market** is especially good during crab season, from **November to February**, when you can find plenty of king and hairy crabs. Some places also offer all-you-can-eat crab meals for around **5000-7000 yen**.

To get to these markets, use the **JR lines**. For **Hakodate**, take the **JR Hakodate Line** to **Hakodate Station**. For **Nijo Market**, take the **Toho Line** or **Namboku Line** to **Odori Station**. To reach **Otaru**, take the **JR Hakodate Line** from **Sapporo** to **Otaru Station**.

5.5.1 TRAIN SYSTEM

Getting around Hokkaido by train is really easy and convenient. If you're heading to major cities like Hakodate, Asahikawa, or Niseko, you'll want to use the **Limited Express Trains** run by JR Hokkaido. For example, to travel from **Sapporo** to **Hakodate**, you can catch the **Limited Express Hokuto**. It's a scenic trip that takes about **3.5 hours**, and the train departs from **Sapporo Station**, which is a central hub that's easy to reach. A one-way ticket costs around **¥8,000**, but if you have a **JR Pass**, you can ride for free. Make sure to enjoy the view, especially during winter when everything is covered in snow.

In the summer heading to **Furano** or **Biei** to see the famous lavender fields, the **Furano Lavender Express** is perfect. You can board at **Sapporo Station** or

Asahikawa Station, and the ride takes about 2 hours. The tickets cost around ¥2,500, or it's included if you have the JR Pass. Once you're there, make sure to visit Farm Tomita for lavender photos and some local soft cream made with Hokkaido's famous milk.

If skiing or snowboarding is your thing, getting to Niseko is simple. Take the JR Hakodate Line from Sapporo to Otaru, then transfer to a local train that goes to Kutchan Station. From there, shuttle buses take you straight to the slopes. The whole trip takes about 2.5 hours, and it costs roughly ¥2,500 for a one-way fare, unless you're using the JR Pass.

For remote places like Shiretoko Peninsula, take the Limited Express Okhotsk from Sapporo or Asahikawa to Abashiri Station. It's about a 5.5-hour ride, and a one-way ticket is around ¥9,000, but it's free with the JR Pass. You'll need to take a local bus or rent a car from there to reach the national park, and renting a car for about ¥7,000 per day might be more flexible, especially in winter when roads can get snowy.

For visiting the Wakkanai, the northernmost city in Japan, take the Limited Express Soya from Asahikawa. The trip takes about 5 hours, and tickets cost around ¥10,000. From Wakkanai Port, you can catch ferries to Rishiri and Rebun Islands, where you can enjoy scenic hikes. Ferry tickets are about ¥5,000 round trip.

Don't forget that the JR Hokkaido Pass is a great deal if you're traveling a lot. For ¥24,000, you can get a 7-day pass that covers all JR trains in Hokkaido. It's a really good option for long trips and makes things a lot easier when you want to explore more than one part of the island.

5.5.2 BEST SEASONAL GEAR AND PACKING TIPS

Packing for Hokkaido, it's all about being prepared for the season you're visiting in. In winter, you'll need to focus on keeping warm because temperatures drop a lot, especially if you're heading to places like Niseko or Furano for skiing. Make sure you pack thermal layers, a thick jacket, snow boots, gloves, and a hat. Niseko is about a 2-hour train or bus ride from New Chitose Airport, and you can easily rent all the ski gear you need there if you don't want to carry it. Rentals usually cost between ¥3000 to ¥7000 per day, depending on what you need. If you're planning to visit in summer, it's the perfect time for hiking. Daisetsuzan National Park is a great spot for hiking, and the trails start from Asahidake Onsen, which you can reach via a bus from Asahikawa Station. Pack light-weight, breathable clothes, a rain jacket, and hiking boots, since the weather can be unpredictable, and make sure to bring sunscreen and a hat for sun protection.

For visiting **onsens** (hot springs) in remote areas, like **Nyuto Onsen** in **Akan National Park**, bring a small bag with essentials like a towel and clean clothes because these spots are all about relaxing in nature. Renting a car is the easiest way to get there, and you can pick one up at **Sapporo Station** or **New Chitose Airport**. If you're visiting in winter, be sure the car has snow tires or chains, as the roads can get icy. To reach **The Blue Pond in Biei**, take the **JR Furano Line** to **Biei Station**, and from there you can take a bus or taxi. It's best to go in the early morning when the light is perfect for photos, and entry is free, which is great if you're looking to save on costs.

For seafood, **Hakodate Morning Market** is a must. It's just a short walk from **Hakodate Station**, and the best time to visit is around **7 AM** when the market is most active. You can grab a fresh seafood bowl (kaisen-don) for **¥2000 to ¥3500**, and try grilled seafood straight from the stalls. The market is also great for picking up fresh ingredients if you're staying in an Airbnb with a kitchen. **Sapporo's Ramen Alley** is another spot you shouldn't miss, especially for **miso ramen**, which is famous in the area. Most bowls cost between **¥800 to ¥1200**, and you can find ramen spots open late at night, perfect after a long day of exploring.

Renting a car to visit beyond the main cities, it's recommended to get one at **Sapporo Station** or **New Chitose Airport**. Prices start from around **¥6000 per day**, and if you're visiting in winter, make sure you get snow tires. For more remote areas like **Shiretoko Peninsula**, car rentals are almost necessary since public transportation is limited.

CHAPTER 6
HIROSHIMA

6.1 HISTORY

6.1.1 WORLD WAR II AND THE ATOMIC BOMBING

On the morning of August 6, 1945, at precisely 8:15 AM, the atomic bomb was dropped, forever altering the landscape and history of the city. **The bomb exploded over the center of Hiroshima, near what is now Peace Memorial Park, wiping out nearly everything within a two-kilometer radius** and killing tens of thousands instantly. By the end of that year, the estimated death toll reached around 140,000, a devastating figure that continues to echo in the memories of the survivors, known as *hibakusha*. They faced not only the immediate destruction but also the long-term suffering from burns, injuries, and radiation sickness.

Today, Hiroshima stands as a **city of resilience and reflection**, located on Japan's Honshu Island, in the Chugoku region, accessible by various forms of transportation. **If you're traveling by train, the easiest route is via the JR Sanyo Shinkansen** (bullet train), which stops at **Hiroshima Station**, about a 10-minute taxi or tram ride from the Peace Memorial Park area. **If you prefer public transport, trams run frequently**—tram number 2 or 6 will take you directly from Hiroshima Station to Genbaku Dome-mae stop, right in front of the Atomic Bomb Dome.

Surrounding the Peace Memorial Park, you'll find plenty of opportunities for reflection, but also daily life—restaurants, cafes, and shops, all rebuilt on what was once a city in ruins. A great local tip is to try the **Hiroshima-style okonomiyaki**, a savory pancake filled with cabbage, noodles, and various toppings, easily found in eateries along the city's main streets, especially around the Okonomimura food village near the city center.

The cost of visiting the Peace Memorial Park is free, though some of the memorials, like the Peace Memorial Museum, charge a small fee (approximately ¥200). **You can spend a few hours or even a whole day exploring the monuments**, including the **Atomic Bomb Dome** (the only building left standing near the bomb's hypocenter), the **Children's Peace Monument**, and the **Peace Flame**, which remains lit until all nuclear weapons are abolished.

6.1.2 REBUILDING AND MODERN HIROSHIMA

Hiroshima's transformation after the atomic bombing stands as a symbol of resilience and peace, and walking through the city today. **The heart of Hiroshima is located in the Chugoku region of Japan and is easily accessible via Hiroshima Station**, which connects to the **JR Sanyo Shinkansen** line. **From Osaka or Kyoto, you can take the bullet train and arrive in Hiroshima in just a few hours.** Once you get there, the **Hiroshima Electric Railway (Hiroden) tram system** is one of the best ways to get around. You'll want to take the **tram line 2 or line 6**, which will bring you directly to **Peace Memorial Park**, one of the key sites to start your exploration of the city's reconstruction and modern vibe.

In **downtown Hiroshima**, the modern city emerges from where ruins once stood. **Peace Boulevard (Heiwa Odori)** is a central road that stretches across the city, and around here you'll find bustling shopping areas, cozy cafes, and a mix of new buildings that symbolize Hiroshima's growth after the war. **Hondori Street**, located near Peace Memorial Park, is the go-to area for shopping, dining, and experiencing modern Hiroshima culture.

To see how Hiroshima was rebuilt, start at **Peace Memorial Park**, which is located along **Otemachi Street**. The park itself is a serene green space designed to reflect on the city's tragic history while showcasing its journey toward peace. Here, you can visit **the Atomic Bomb Dome**, which was left as a ruin to serve as a reminder of the destruction, surrounded by the rebuilt city. Entrance to the park is free, but if you want to dive deeper into history, you can visit the **Hiroshima Peace Memorial Museum** for a small fee (200 yen). The museum gives you a profound insight into the bombing, its aftermath, and the city's efforts in promoting world peace. It's open from **8:30 a.m. to 6:00 p.m.**, with extended hours during summer.

Is also famous for its **okonomiyaki,** a savory pancake layered with noodles and cabbage. Head over to **Okonomimura**, located on **Shintenchi Street,** near **Hatchobori Station,** which is easily reachable by tram. The area is packed with small eateries where you can watch the chefs cook right in front of you. Prices for a filling okonomiyaki meal are around **800–1200 yen.**

Around **Hiroshima Station,** you'll also find a variety of izakayas and casual restaurants offering local seafood and **Hiroshima-style tsukemen (spicy cold noodles).** For those interested in sake, **Saijo** is a sake-brewing district located just a short **train ride on the JR Kure Line from Hiroshima Station.**

Hiroshima Station is a hub for reaching **Miyajima Island,** famous for its **floating torii gate** and **Itsukushima Shrine.** You can take the **JR Sanyo Line** to **Miyajimaguchi Station** and hop on a ferry to the island. Ferry rides cost about **180 yen** one way, and the island itself is ideal for a peaceful afternoon of exploring sacred shrines, hiking trails, and enjoying views of the Seto Inland Sea.

6.2.1 PEACE MEMORIAL PARK

Peace Memorial Park is located at **1-2 Nakajima-cho, Naka Ward, Hiroshima,** right at the heart of the city where the atomic bomb was dropped. To reach the park, you can take a tram from **Hiroshima Station** on lines **2** or **6** and get off at the **Genbaku Dome-mae** stop. The ride takes about **15 minutes**, and the fare costs around **¥180**. Alternatively, it's a pleasant walk from the station, taking around **20 to 30 minutes**, with scenic views along the way. The area is also well-serviced by buses if you prefer that route.

Once you're at the park, the **Atomic Bomb Dome** is one of the first things you'll see, standing as a haunting reminder of the devastation that took place here. It's one of **Hiroshima's most iconic landmarks**, a preserved building that survived the blast. You can explore the park freely as it's open 24 hours and **doesn't require an entrance fee**. The entire park was designed to be a place of reflection and peace, so take your time walking along the paths.

The **Hiroshima Peace Memorial Museum** is within the park, and its **entrance fee is ¥200**. It's open from **8:30 AM to 6:00 PM** (though hours may vary during peak seasons), and it's highly recommended to visit this museum to get a deeper understanding of the bombing and its impact. The museum contains artifacts and detailed exhibits that will give you more insight into what happened during and after the atomic bombing.

You'll find the **Children's Peace Monument** dedicated to Sadako Sasaki, who became a symbol of hope and peace after folding 1,000 paper cranes. People from all over the world send paper cranes to this spot, making it one of the park's most emotionally moving areas.

The **Peace Flame**, which burns continuously, symbolizes a world without nuclear weapons. It's a simple yet powerful sight that you'll pass as you walk through the park. The flame will stay lit until all nuclear weapons are eradicated, reminding visitors of the park's broader message of global peace.

After your visit, there are some great casual spots around the park, especially on **Heiwa Odori Avenue**, which runs along the edge of the park. You can try local favorites like **okonomiyaki** (Hiroshima-style savory pancakes) at nearby restaurants, which usually cost around **¥1,000 to ¥1,500** per dish. Popular places like **Okonomimura** are a short tram ride away, offering a range of choices. The best time to visit the park is either early morning, when the atmosphere is calm and reflective, or late afternoon, when the sunset adds a golden glow to the surroundings. If you're looking for a quieter time, avoid major national holidays and weekends when the park tends to attract larger crowds.

6.2.2 MIYAJIMA ISLAND

To reach **Miyajima Island**, you'll first need to take a train to **Miyajimaguchi Station**, which is located on the **JR Sanyo Line**. From **Hiroshima Station**, it takes around **30 minutes**, and the trains run frequently throughout the day. Once you arrive at the station, the **Miyajimaguchi Pier** is only a **five-minute walk** away, and ferries to the island run every **15 minutes**. The ferry ride itself takes just **10 minutes** and costs about **¥180** for a one-way trip. During the ferry ride, you'll get a perfect view of the **Floating Torii Gate**, especially as you approach the island.

Once on **Miyajima Island**, start by visiting the iconic **Itsukushima Shrine**, which is just a short walk from the ferry terminal. The shrine is known for its dramatic positioning over the water, and entrance costs ¥300 for adults. If the tide is low, you can walk right up to the **Torii Gate**, but during high tide, it appears to float. As you explore, you'll encounter **friendly deer** that freely roam the island—though be cautious as they are curious and might try to eat anything you're carrying. For hiking enthusiasts, take the trail up **Mount Misen** for spectacular views of the island and the **Seto Inland Sea**. The **Mount Misen ropeway** offers an easier way up for ¥1,000 one way or ¥1,800 round trip, but if you prefer hiking, the trail takes about **90 minutes** to reach the summit. Don't miss visiting the **Misen Hondo** and **Reikado Hall** near the top. After exploring, stop by local food stalls to try **momiji manju**, a maple leaf-shaped pastry filled with sweet bean paste, or enjoy fresh **oysters**, which are a local delicacy.

6.3.1 HIROSHIMA-STYLE OKONOMIYAKI

In Hiroshima, trying **Hiroshima-style okonomiyaki** is a must, especially if you're near **Okonomimura**, located on **5-13 Shintenchi**, a short walk from **Hatchobori Station**, where you can take tram lines 1, 2, or 6, with trams running every 10 minutes, costing ¥190 for a one-way fare. When you step into Okonomimura, the experience is both interactive and satisfying as you watch the chefs layer the batter, cabbage, pork, and noodles—distinctly different from the mixed Osaka-style version—on a hotplate right in front of you, with a final egg layer on top. This savory pancake is then topped with okonomiyaki sauce, mayonnaise, and a sprinkle of optional toppings like dried seaweed or bonito flakes. Prices generally range from **¥1,000 to ¥1,500**, depending on where you dine and the number of toppings you choose. Another highly recommended spot to try this iconic dish is **Nagata-ya**, situated near **Otemachi** on **1-7-19 Otemachi**, conveniently close to the **Atomic Bomb Dome** and **Peace Memorial Park**. From **Hondori Station**, you can either take a short walk or hop on a tram to reach this famous restaurant, where you can enjoy watching the chef cook right in front of you, ensuring a fresh and personalized meal.

After indulging in okonomiyaki, a 10-minute stroll will take you to the **Shukkeien Garden**, a tranquil spot for relaxation, or to **Hiroshima Castle**, where you can explore its reconstructed keep and learn about the city's history before and after the atomic bombing. If you're planning to make it a longer day trip, Miyajima Island is a 30-minute train and ferry ride away, offering a chance to see the famous **floating torii gate** and hike up **Mount Misen**. For another meal, you can stop by **Reichan**, near **Hiroshima Station**, where okonomiyaki is served in a more traditional setting, with prices around **¥900 to ¥1,400**, and the restaurant's long history dating back to the 1950s offers an authentic, nostalgic atmosphere. Don't miss the chance to pair your meal with a glass of locally brewed **Hiroshima sake**, available at most izakayas in the area.

6.3.2 LOCAL IZAKAYAS AND EATERIES

Head to **Nagarekawa District**. This area is filled with small restaurants and bars, perfect for a night of local food and drinks. You can get here by taking tram line **1** or **6** to **Chuden-mae Station**, and from there it's just a short walk to streets like **Nagarekawa-cho** or **Yagenbori-dori**, where you'll find cozy spots like **Yakitori Saikai** or **Sakaba Goma**. These places are famous for serving **Hiroshima-style okonomiyaki**, grilled meats, and seafood, all in a warm, welcoming atmosphere with low wooden tables and soft lighting. Meals here usually cost around **¥2,000– ¥4,000**, making it a great place for both a casual dinner and drinks.

For something quieter, you have to visit **Hatchobori**, just a short tram ride from **Hiroshima Station**. Take tram line **1** to **Hatchobori Station**, and in a couple of minutes, you'll find streets like **Ebisu-dori**, where you can try izakayas like **Nagaoka Ebisu** or **Tsubokura**. These places specialize in seasonal seafood like fried **oysters** and **grilled fish**, and a meal with drinks will cost you around **¥3,000–¥5,000**. Hatchobori is great for enjoying a more laid-back evening with locals, and it's a good spot to try **sake** along with your meal.

For sake traditional taste, take a JR train from **Hiroshima Station** to **Saijo**, which is about **40 minutes** away. Saijo is famous for its sake breweries like **Kamoizumi** and **Hakubotan**, and you'll find izakayas attached to these breweries where you can try local sake along with dishes like **salt-grilled fish** or **miso-marinated meats**. Meals here usually cost around **¥3,000 to ¥5,000**, depending on how much sake you drink. This area offers a quieter, more traditional vibe, perfect for those who enjoy exploring local food and drink culture.

Back in central Hiroshima, the **Fukuromachi** area is another great place for a modern izakaya experience. Just a short walk from **Kamiyacho-nishi Station** (tram lines **1** and **3**), you'll find trendy izakayas like **Kaeru**, which serves both traditional dishes like **okonomiyaki** and fusion foods that mix Japanese and Western flavors. Prices in this area are a bit higher, with meals costing around **¥4,000** or more, but the atmosphere is lively, often with open kitchens and outdoor seating, making it a great spot to spend an evening with friends.

6.4.1 SHIMANAMI KAIDO CYCLING ROUTE

The **Shimanami Kaido Cycling Route**, located between **Onomichi** in **Hiroshima Prefecture** and **Imabari** in **Ehime Prefecture** on **Shikoku Island**, is one of Japan's most stunning long-distance bike routes. It spans **70 kilometers** and takes you across six islands via seven bridges, offering unparalleled views of the **Seto Inland Sea**. You can begin your journey at **Onomichi**, a coastal town easily accessible by **JR trains** (approximately **90 minutes** from **Hiroshima Station** via the **JR Sanyo Line**). From **Onomichi Station**, it's a short walk to **Onomichi Port**, where you'll find the **Shimanami Japan bike rental center** on **2-9 Higashigoshocho**. Bike rentals range from **¥1,000 to ¥3,000** depending on the type, with electric-assist bikes being perfect for a more relaxed ride.

It's recommended to start the day early in the morning, particularly during **spring** (April to May) and **autumn** (September to October), when the weather is pleasant and ideal for cycling. The first bridge you'll encounter is the **Innoshima Bridge**, leading to **Mukaishima Island**, where you'll enjoy peaceful coastal paths and views of the islands ahead. The route is marked with clear blue lines to guide cyclists. The trip continues across several breathtaking bridges like the **Tatara Bridge**, which is the longest cable-stayed bridge on the route and provides stunning panoramic views of the Seto Inland Sea.

For breaks and food, **Setoda** on **Ikuchi Island** is a must-stop spot. Here you can visit the **Kosanji Temple**, a colorful and ornate complex, and the nearby **Hirayama Ikuo Museum of Art**. Setoda is famous for its citrus products, especially its lemons, and many local eateries offer **lemon-infused dishes**. Look for small restaurants like **Shima Kitchen** on **Setoda Hirakiyacho Street** to enjoy a local meal, with prices ranging from **¥1,000 to ¥2,000** for fresh seafood or udon. As you cycle further, you'll come across **Omishima Island**, home to the **Oyamazumi Shrine**, a site with deep historical importance, housing a treasure trove of samurai armor. The islands offer peaceful scenery, dotted with small fishing villages and quiet temples, giving you a break from the more commercialized tourist paths. Ferries are available between some islands if you'd like to explore other areas more leisurely, with ferry rides costing around **¥500 to ¥1,000** depending on the route.

The final leg of the route leads you to **Imabari**, where you can return your bike at one of the rental stations. Imabari is famous for its **towel factories** and the impressive **Imabari Castle**, a unique seaside castle that you might want to visit before heading back. Imabari Station is connected to the **JR Yosan Line**, making it easy to catch a train back toward Hiroshima or other destinations.

With bike-friendly accommodations scattered across the islands, such as

Cyclo no Ie in **Setoda**, priced around ¥5,000 to ¥8,000 per night, the **Shimanami Kaido** is perfect for either a one-day challenge

6.4.2 BEST SUNSET SPOTS

To get to **Ninoshima Island**, you'll need to take the **Hiroden Tram Line 1** from **Hiroshima Station** to **Ujina Port**, a trip that takes about **30 minutes**. From there, hop on a ferry that costs around **¥1,800 round trip** and takes another **30 minutes** to cross to the island. Once you're there, head to **Ninoshima Beach**, a quiet spot where you can relax and watch the sunset over the **Seto Inland Sea**. The best time to visit is between **May and September** when the weather is warmer. You can also grab a bite from one of the local seafood shacks nearby that offer dishes like **grilled oysters** and **anago** (conger eel), which typically cost between **¥500 and ¥1,200**.

Another great spot for watching the sunset is **Tomo no Ura**, a historic port town. Take the **JR Sanyo Line** from **Hiroshima Station** to **Fukuyama Station** (about **1 hour**), then a **30-minute** bus ride to **Tomo Port**. From there, you can take a short ferry ride (around **¥240**) to **Sensuijima Island**, where you can hike to **Mount Jōyama**. The view from the top, especially during late summer, is amazing as the sun sets over the **Seto Inland Sea**. While in the area, you can enjoy a local specialty, **tai-meshi** (sea bream rice), at one of the restaurants around Tomo no Ura, with meals costing between **¥1,500 and ¥2,500**.

Then visit **Mitaki-dera Temple**. Take the **Yokogawa Line** from **Hiroshima Station** to **Mitaki Station** (about **20 minutes**), then walk up to the temple. Surrounded by nature, this place is especially beautiful in autumn when the leaves change color. The temple's peaceful atmosphere is perfect for watching the sunset. After exploring, you can stop by a tea house near the entrance and enjoy **matcha tea** and traditional sweets for around **¥500**.

For a grand view, go to **Miyajima Island** and take the **JR Sanyo Line** to **Miyajimaguchi Station** (about **30 minutes** from Hiroshima), then catch the ferry to the island (about **¥180** one way). Once on the island, take the **Miyajima Ropeway** to **Shishiiwa Observatory** for around **¥2,000 round trip**. The view of the sunset from the top of **Mount Misen** is breathtaking, especially in late spring or early autumn. After coming down, stroll along **Omotesando Street** and try **momiji manju** (maple leaf-shaped cakes) or grilled oysters, with prices ranging from **¥200 to ¥600**.

CHAPTER 7
OKINAWA

7.1 OVERVIEW

7.1.1 OKINAWA AND RYUKYU CULTURE

Okinawa, located about 1,600 kilometers southwest of Tokyo, can be reached by a direct flight from major cities in Japan, including **Tokyo's Haneda Airport** and **Osaka's Kansai International Airport**. Once you land at **Naha Airport**, the main gateway to the island, public transport options are straightforward. From the airport, you can take the **Yui Rail**, Okinawa's monorail system, which runs from the airport into the city center of **Naha**—this is the best way to reach key sites like **Kokusai Street**, known for shopping, restaurants, and entertainment. Buses are also available, though renting a car is highly recommended, as it gives you flexibility, especially when exploring further afield areas like the north or east coasts. Okinawa's public transportation system can be slow, particularly when navigating rural areas, so plan accordingly.

The **Ryukyu Kingdom** was a powerful trading nation from the 15th to the 19th century, and you can explore its history by visiting **Shurijo Castle**, the former seat of the Ryukyu kings. It's located in the **Shuri district** of Naha, easily accessible by the Yui Rail's **Shuri Station**. The castle grounds have been partially rebuilt after a devastating fire in 2019, but the area remains an important symbol of Okinawan culture and pride. Entrance fees are around **820 yen** for adults, and the site is open from **8:30 AM to 5:30 PM** most days. As you walk through the castle grounds, you'll get a clear sense of Okinawa's unique architecture, which merges Chinese, Japanese, and indigenous styles.

After visiting historical sites, a walk down **Kokusai Street** (also known as **International Street**) is a must. This bustling area is full of eateries where you can sample traditional **Okinawan dishes**. Head to **Makishi Public Market** for a fresh, authentic experience where local vendors sell everything from **soki soba** (a local noodle soup with pork ribs) to **goya champuru** (a stir-fry dish made with bitter melon, tofu, and pork). Prices for meals range from **700 yen to 1,500 yen**, and if you're adventurous, try the **taco rice**, a fusion dish unique to Okinawa that blends Mexican-style taco toppings with rice. You'll find many restaurants scattered along Kokusai Street, but if you're seeking a quieter meal, the nearby **Tsuboya Pottery District** offers hidden gems with a more traditional atmosphere. Expect meals in the mid-range, around **1,000 to 2,000 yen**, depending on what you order.

Outside the city, a visit to the **Okinawa Churaumi Aquarium** on the Motobu Peninsula is highly recommended, especially if you're traveling with family. The aquarium is accessible by car in about **two hours** from Naha, or you can take an express bus from **Naha Bus Terminal**. Tickets cost around **1,880 yen** for adults. Nearby, you can explore the stunning **Emerald Beach**, where snorkeling and swimming are ideal for all ages, and rental gear is available for around **1,500 yen**. For the **rural culture**, head to **Taketomi Island**, accessible via a **ferry from Ishigaki Island**, which takes about **15 minutes**. Here, you can rent a bicycle and roam the streets lined with **traditional Ryukyu houses**, with coral stone walls and red-tiled roofs, which have been preserved in their original form. A ferry ride from **Ishigaki Port** costs around **1,500 yen round trip**.

7.2 TOP BEACHES AND SNORKELING SPOTS

7.2.1 BEST BEACHES ON OKINAWA'S MAIN ISLAND

Emerald Beach is located within the **Okinawa Ocean Expo Park** at **424 Ishikawa, Motobu, Kunigami District**, it's one of the most accessible and family-friendly beaches on **Okinawa's Main Island**, known for its sheltered, crystal-clear waters and soft, white sands. To get there, you can take the **Yanbaru**

Express Bus from **Naha Bus Terminal**, which departs roughly every hour, and get off at the **Kinen Koen-mae Bus Stop**. From the bus stop, it's just a short walk to the beach entrance, which makes it extremely convenient for tourists using public transport. If you're driving, it's about **2 hours** from **Naha Airport** via **National Route 58**, and there's plenty of parking available on-site. The beach is especially popular for families due to the calm waters and snorkeling-friendly conditions, with gear rentals available nearby for around **1,500 yen**. The best time to visit is either early morning, before the afternoon crowds roll in, or later in the afternoon when the light softens, making it an ideal spot for relaxing while also being safe for kids to enjoy.

Around the beach, you'll find the **Okinawa Churaumi Aquarium**, which is one of the most popular attractions on the island, offering a chance to explore marine life both in the sea and at the aquarium. There are also small food stalls nearby selling Okinawan specialties like **soki soba** (Okinawan noodle soup with pork ribs), which usually costs around **800 yen**, and **taco rice**, a local favorite priced at around **700 to 1,000 yen**. These spots are casual but give a real taste of local flavors. It's worth spending a full day here, as the beach's proximity to the park makes it perfect for a blend of nature and culture.

For a more tranquil day, head over to **Zampa Beach**, located at **Uza, Yomitan Village**, near the famous **Cape Zampa Lighthouse**. This beach is especially serene and often quieter than some of the more touristy beaches, making it perfect for a peaceful day out. By public transport, you can take a bus from **Naha Bus Terminal** to the **Zanpa Misaki Iriguchi Bus Stop**, which is about a **15-minute walk** from the beach. For those driving, it takes about **90 minutes from Naha** along **Prefectural Road 6**, and there's parking available nearby. Snorkeling equipment can be rented for about **1,200 yen**, and you'll also find showers and changing rooms, making it a convenient option for families or those staying all day.

Nearby attractions include **Cape Zampa Lighthouse**, where you can enjoy panoramic views of the coast for a small entrance fee of **200 yen**, and for a more immersive experience, try visiting one of the cafes near **Cape Zampa**, which offer Okinawan dishes like **chanpuru** (stir-fried vegetables and tofu) or fresh **seafood bowls**, typically priced at **1,000 to 1,500 yen**.

7.3 CULTURAL AND HISTORICAL LANDMARKS

7.3.1 SHURIJO CASTLE

Shurijo Castle, located at **1 Chome-2 Shurikinjocho, Naha, Okinawa**, is a must-visit site for anyone interested in Okinawa's rich history and the legacy of the **Ryukyu Kingdom**. To reach the castle, the easiest option is taking the **Yui Rail** from central Naha to **Shuri Station**. From there, it's a **15-minute uphill walk**, and you can follow well-marked signs leading directly to the castle. There's a convenient parking area near the castle grounds, with prices around **300 yen per hour**.

The castle itself, though still under reconstruction following the 2019 fire, offers a profound look into **Okinawa's historical importance as a center of culture and diplomacy**. The **outer gates**, such as the **Kankaimon Gate**, still stand strong, giving you a glimpse of the elaborate **Ryukyu architecture**, which blends elements of both **Chinese and Japanese influence**. When you pass through these gates, you immediately sense the power that this site once held as the political heart of the **Ryukyu Kingdom**. Exploring the **castle grounds**, you'll find plaques and information about the ongoing reconstruction efforts, which are part of a national initiative to restore this **UNESCO World Heritage Site** to its former glory. The guided tours, which run regularly throughout the day, provide deeper insight into the **Ryukyu Dynasty's role** as a bridge between **China, Japan, and Southeast Asia**. English-language guides are available and highly recommended to fully appreciate the historical context.

It's best to arrive early, especially around **8:30 AM** or later in the afternoon, to avoid the busiest hours. The **castle grounds are open from 8 AM to 6:30 PM** (times may vary during reconstruction), and admission is about **820 yen** for adults. After visiting the castle, take time to explore the nearby **Shurikinjocho Stone Path**, an ancient stone road that used to connect Shuri with the rest of the island. The **peaceful scenery** of this area is often less crowded, allowing for a more reflective walk through **Okinawa's natural beauty**.

For lunch or dinner, head to **Shuri Soba**, located just a short walk from the castle on **Kinjo-cho Street**, where you can enjoy a traditional bowl of **Okinawan soba** for about **800-1,200 yen**. The broth here is rich, made with pork and dashi, and it's served with thick, chewy noodles that are unique to the region. Alternatively, for a more refined experience, try **Sui Dunchi**, an **Okinawan cuisine restaurant** housed in a **traditional Ryukyu-style building**, offering dishes like **rafute** (braised pork belly) and **goya champuru** (stir-fried bitter melon), with meals typically costing around **2,000 to 4,000 yen** per person. If you're in the mood for something lighter, stop by **Shuri Ryusen**, where you can enjoy **Okinawan tea** and snacks such as **sata andagi** for about **500-800 yen**.

Nearby attractions, **Tamaudun Mausoleum**, located just a **5-minute walk from the castle**, is another historically significant site, where members of the **Ryukyu royal family** are entombed. The entrance fee is around **300 yen**, and it provides a solemn reminder of the island's royal heritage. Visiting **Shurijo Castle** during the fall, particularly in **late October**, aligns with the **Shuri Castle Festival**, where reenactments of **traditional court ceremonies** take place, accompanied by **costumed parades and performances**, bringing the rich history of the **Ryukyu Dynasty** to life in a way that no written history can capture.

7.3.2 TRADITIONAL EISA DANCES

Eisa dances are a huge part of Okinawan culture, especially during the Obon Festival, when they honor the spirits of ancestors. These performances combine powerful drumming, chanting, and dancing, with performers dressed in bright, traditional costumes. One of the best places to watch Eisa is the Okinawa Zento Eisa Festival in Okinawa City, held at Koza Sports Park in late August. To get there from Naha, take the express bus number 23 from Naha Bus Terminal near Kokusai Street, which runs every 20-30 minutes and costs around 600 yen. The ride is about 45 minutes. If you're driving, it's an easy trip on the expressway, but parking fills up fast, especially if you arrive late in the afternoon, as performances usually start around 6 PM. Smaller Eisa performances can be seen in village squares in Uruma City or in Naha along Kokusai Street during the Obon period. After watching, try some local street food like sata andagi, a sweet Okinawan doughnut that costs about 150 yen each, or stop by Shimujo restaurant on Shurikinjocho Street near Shurijo Castle for goya champuru, priced between 800-1,000 yen. For an even deeper experience, you can join a workshop at the Okinawa Prefectural Museum and Art Museum on Omoromachi Street in Naha, where you'll learn the basics of Eisa for a fee of 1,000-2,000 yen. The museum is easy to reach by taking the Okinawa Monorail (Yui Rail) to Omoromachi Station. Participating in a workshop gives you a chance to really connect with Okinawan culture through dance.

7.4 HIDDEN ISLAND ADVENTURES

7.4.1 FERRY TO OKINAWA'S SMALLER ISLANDS

For lesser-known islands, head to **Tomari Port** in **Naha City**, which is located at **3-25-1 Maejima, Naha, Okinawa**, easily reachable via **Asahibashi Station** on the **Yui Rail** line. You can either walk 15 minutes from the station to the port or take a short taxi ride. The ferries departing from here connect you to some of the quieter islands in the **Kerama Islands**, such as **Tokashiki** and **Zamami**. Ferries to **Tokashiki Island** typically depart at **7:00 AM, 10:00 AM**, and in the afternoon at **3:30 PM**, with ticket prices around **2,500 yen one way**. The journey takes approximately **35 minutes** on the high-speed ferry or **70 minutes** on the slower, more scenic boat.

Once on **Tokashiki Island**, head to **Aharen Beach**, which is a short bus ride from the ferry terminal; the buses are timed to coincide with ferry arrivals. Here, you can rent snorkeling gear at the beach for **1,500 yen**, allowing you to explore the stunning coral reefs right off the shore. After snorkeling, you can relax at one of the local eateries lining the beach—places like **Aharen Café** offer light meals such as **taco rice** for about **900 yen**. If you're more interested in hiking, there's a popular trail leading to **Aharen Observatory**, offering panoramic views of the coast.

If you want to visit **Zamami Island**, the ferry departs from Tomari Port as well, with tickets costing about **3,000 yen one way**, and the journey lasts about **50 minutes**. Once there, **Furuzamami Beach**, located a short bus ride from the ferry terminal, offers a more tranquil experience. You'll find local shops renting bicycles for **1,500 yen per day**, giving you the freedom to explore the island at your own pace. As you bike around, you might stumble upon local spots serving **soki soba**, a traditional Okinawan noodle dish, typically priced around **1,000 yen**, offering an authentic taste of island life.

For something more spiritual, **Kudaka Island**, known as the **Island of the Gods**, offers a unique, quieter adventure. To get there, take the ferry from **Azama Port** in **Nanjo City**, a **30-minute bus ride** from **Shuri Station** on the **Yui Rail**, followed by a short walk. The ferry to Kudaka Island costs around **1,500 yen round-trip**, and the journey itself is only **15 minutes**. Once you arrive, Kudaka Island is best explored on foot or by bike, which can be rented from local shops for about **1,200 yen per day**. You can enjoy the peaceful landscapes, traditional Okinawan homes, and spiritual sites. Stop by small eateries like **Kudaka Teahouse** where they serve simple dishes like **goya champuru** for 800 yen—an affordable and refreshing meal in the midst of your island exploration.

7.4.2 TROPICAL HIKES AND WATERFALLS

Visitig the **Yanbaru Forest** in northern **Okinawa's Main Island**, you'll be surrounded by lush greenery, hidden waterfalls, and peaceful trails. To get there, you can take a bus from **Naha Bus Terminal** to **Nago City**, using bus #20 or #120, which takes about two hours. After that, switch to a local bus toward **Oku** or **Hentona**, closer to the forest, but renting a car is easier and faster since it gives you more freedom to explore different spots.

One of the best places to start is the hike to **Hiji Falls** in **Kunigami Village**. The trail is about 1.5 kilometers long, an easy walk with beautiful views, including a suspension bridge. You can take the **Hentona-bound bus** from **Nago** and get off at **Hiji Falls Iriguchi Bus Stop**. It's a short walk from there to the trailhead, and the entrance fee is **500 yen**. Going early in the morning is a good idea to avoid crowds, and don't forget to bring water, sunscreen, and insect repellent since it's a tropical area with a lot of wildlife.

If you want something quieter, try the trail to **Taa Waterfall** near **Ogimi Village**. It's more remote, so joining a guided eco-tour is the best way to get there. Tours usually cost around **5,000 yen** and include transport, making it easier to find the waterfall and enjoy a peaceful swim. There won't be many tourists around, so it's perfect if you want to escape the crowds.

After your hike, you can grab a meal at **Yanbaru Soba** along **Route 58** in **Kunigami Village**. They serve traditional Okinawan soba, and it's only **800 to 1,200 yen** for a tasty, filling bowl. If you still have energy, **Daisekirinzan**, near

Cape Hedo, is another great place to visit. It's about a 30-minute drive from **Hiji Falls** on **Route 70**, and the limestone rock formations and ocean views are stunning. Admission is **820 yen**, and the trails are easy to walk.

You'll likely spot some unique wildlife along the way, like the rare **Yanbaru kuina**, a bird found only in this region.

CHAPTER 8
FESTIVALS AND SPECIAL EVENTS

8.1 TRADITIONAL FESTIVALS

8.1.1 AWA ODORI DANCE FESTIVAL

The **Awa Odori Dance Festival** happens in **Tokushima City**, on **Shikoku Island**, and it's the biggest dance festival in Japan. You can get there by taking the **JR train** from **Osaka** or **Kyoto** straight to **Tokushima Station**, which is located on **Terashima Honcho Nishi Street**. Public transportation during the festival is extended, so buses and trains run later into the night. Once you arrive, the main event area is along **National Route 192**, and you can buy tickets to watch the dancers from **paid stands** near the station, which usually cost between **¥1,500 and ¥2,500**. If you prefer a more relaxed, free viewing, just head to the side streets, like **Shinmachi River Street**, where you'll still see plenty of performances in a more casual setting.

You can also join the dancing by renting traditional **yukata** or **happi coats** from stalls near **Aibahama Park**. The cost for renting these outfits is usually between **¥3,000 to ¥5,000**. The main dancing happens in the evening, so it's a good idea to arrive by **5 p.m.** to find a spot before the streets get crowded. After the festival, there are lots of food stalls selling things like **yakitori** and **Tokushima ramen** for around **¥700 to ¥1,000**. There are also small shops offering sweet treats like **warabimochi** for about **¥300**. You'll want to grab something to eat as you watch or after you've danced. For a quieter place to visit during the day, **Bizan Park** is just a short walk from the festival and gives you a great view of the city and the mountains. You can also visit the **Tokushima Castle Ruins** in **Tokushima Central Park** nearby, which is a peaceful green space to take a break before all the festivities start. After the festival, try a local izakaya like **Izakaya Gankozushi** on **Nakajo Dori Street**, where you can enjoy fresh seafood and local sake for about ¥3,000 to ¥5,000 per person, perfect for unwinding after the excitement of the day.

8.1.2 SUMMER FIREWORKS FESTIVALS

During Japan's **summer fireworks festivals**, the **Sumida River Fireworks Festival** in Tokyo is one of the most popular events, and it takes place along the **Sumida River** near **Asakusa Station** on the **Ginza and Asakusa subway lines**. This event lights up the skies above **Sumida Park** and the surrounding riverside areas. To get there, you'll want to arrive at **Asakusa Station** early—at least **four to five hours before** the fireworks begin at around **7:00 PM**—to secure a prime viewing spot. Streets along the river, especially **Taito Ward**, are filled with festival stalls where you can grab classic festival foods like **yakisoba**, **okonomiyaki**, and **taiyaki**—with prices ranging between ¥500 to ¥1,200. For an even better view, reserved seating is available around ¥2,000 to ¥3,000 per person, offering closer proximity to the river, where the reflections of fireworks dance on the water, enhancing the overall spectacle.

Moving north to Niigata, the **Nagaoka Fireworks Festival** takes place along the banks of the **Shinano River** near **Nagaoka Station** on the **Joetsu Shinkansen** line, with access to the festival being incredibly convenient. The fireworks typically start at **7:30 PM** and go on for about two hours, with some of the largest fireworks displays in the country. Arriving around **mid-afternoon** will give you enough time to settle along the river, and there's plenty to do while you wait, including exploring food stalls offering local Niigata specialties like **Nagaoka-style ramen** and grilled seafood, which range from ¥600 to ¥1,500. After the fireworks, expect some congestion at **Nagaoka Station**, so either head there immediately or linger longer to avoid the rush.

In **Akita Prefecture**, the **Omagari Fireworks Competition** takes place along the **Omonogawa River** in **Daisen City**, which is accessible via **Omagari Station** on the **Akita Shinkansen**. The competition draws a crowd but has a more intimate feel compared to the larger festivals. Fireworks start at **5:00 PM**, but the real show begins after sunset. Arriving at **3:00 PM** gives you plenty of time to find a spot along the river or rent a viewing chair for ¥2,000. Food vendors set up stalls offering local delicacies like **kiritanpo (grilled rice sticks)** and **Akita's famous sake**, with prices typically around **¥500 to ¥1,200**. After the fireworks, the nearby **Omagari Station** is just a short walk, and extra trains are scheduled for the event, though waiting a little after the show is often the best way to avoid the crowds.

8.1.3 GION MATSURI IN KYOTO

Gion Matsuri takes place right in the center of Kyoto, mainly along **Shijo-dori** and **Karasuma-dori** in **Nakagyo Ward**. To get there, you can take the **Keihan Line** to Gion-Shijo Station, or use the **Hankyu Line** to **Karasuma Station**. If you're coming from farther away, **Kyoto Station** on the **JR Line** is your best bet, but it can get crowded during the festival. The main parades happen on **July 17th** and **July 24th**, starting around **9:00 AM**, so it's best to show up by **7:30 AM** to get a good spot along **Shijo-dori** or Oike-dori, which fill up quickly. If you want to see the floats at night, the **Yoiyama nights** on **July 16th** and **23rd** are perfect, with streets closing to traffic and the floats lit up by lanterns.

You'll find plenty of food stalls along **Shijo-dori** and **Kawaramachi-dori** selling festival favorites like **yakitori** (chicken skewers) and **taiyaki** (fish-shaped cakes). Prices range from **¥400 to ¥800**, and if you're looking for a sit-down meal, head over to **Pontocho Alley**, which is close to **Gion-Shijo Station**, for some great **kaiseki** meals, though they can range from **¥2,000 to ¥10,000**. The best viewing spots for the parade are along **Shijo-dori** and **Oike-dori**, but try to avoid **Shijo-Karasuma** intersection after **5:00 PM**, as it gets incredibly packed.

If you need a break from the crowds, head to **Rokuharamitsu-ji Temple**, about 15 minutes from **Gion-Shijo Station**, with a quiet garden and entry at **¥500**. Another peaceful option is **Maruyama Park**, located just a short walk from **Yasaka Shrine**, where you can relax in nature. After the parade, getting back can be tricky because trains will be crowded. You might want to wait it out and grab a late dinner or stroll along the **Kamo River**, where you can enjoy a quieter atmosphere. Taxis are available, but expect long waits. Staying nearby in a **machiya guesthouse** is also a great way to soak up the traditional atmosphere, with prices ranging from **¥10,000 to ¥25,000** per night.

8.1.4 SAPPORO SNOW FESTIVAL

The **Sapporo Snow Festival** as you know already is held every February in **Odori Park** and **Susukino**, both located in the center of Sapporo. To get to **Odori Park**, you can take the subway to **Odori Station** on the **Namboku, Tozai,** or **Toho lines**, or walk from **Sapporo Station**, which is about **10 minutes away**. If you head to **Susukino**, you'll be on the **Namboku Line**, and the stop is **Susukino Station**, just a short ride from Odori.

In **Odori Park**, you'll see giant snow sculptures, some over **10 meters tall**. It's a great idea to come in the evening around **5:00 PM**, as the sculptures are lit up and look amazing at night. **Susukino** also hosts beautiful ice sculptures, and there's the famous **Sapporo Ice Bar**, where you can enjoy drinks in ice glasses for around **¥1,000**. Don't forget to stop by **Susukino's food stalls** for local treats like **grilled lamb**, which costs about **¥1,500 per plate**. To visit the festival, public transport is your best option. Trains run until **11:30 PM**, so after the evening light-ups, you'll have plenty of time to get back to your hotel. Most visitors take the **Sapporo Subway—Odori Station** and **Susukino Station** are the key stops you'll use.

The festival itself started in **1950** with some high school students building snow statues, and now it's one of Japan's biggest winter events. You can warm up with local foods like **miso ramen** or grilled seafood from nearby stalls, with prices ranging from **¥500 to ¥1,500**. Don't forget to visit the **Sapporo TV Tower**, close to **Odori Park**, for great views of the snow sculptures. The **observation deck** costs about **¥720** and gives you a bird's-eye view of the whole park.

8.2 MODERN CELEBRATIONS

8.2.1 TOKYO GAME SHOW

The **Tokyo Game Show** happens at **Makuhari Messe**, located at **2-1 Nakase, Mihama Ward, Chiba**. To get there, you can take the **Keiyo Line** from **Tokyo Station** to **Kaihin-Makuhari Station**, which is a **5-minute walk** from the venue. The train ride takes about **30 minutes** and costs around **¥500** one way. Trains run often, so you won't have trouble finding one. If you want to avoid big crowds, try traveling outside rush hours, which are usually from **8:00 AM to 9:30 AM** and **5:00 PM to 7:00 PM**.

Tickets for public days (Saturday and Sunday) cost around **¥2,000 to ¥3,000**. You should buy them early, either online or at convenience stores like **Lawson** or **7-Eleven**. It's best to arrive by **9:00 AM** because the show opens at **10:00 AM**, and popular booths can have long lines. When you get there, you'll find big booths from companies like **Nintendo, Sony**, and **Square Enix**, showing off the latest games. For popular booths, you might wait up to **60-90 minutes** to try out a game, but it's worth it to experience new releases early.

If you're into **cosplay**, there's a dedicated area for it, and you can even dress up yourself. They have **changing rooms** and **lockers** for your stuff, which cost around ¥500. When you need a break, there are **food courts** inside with bento boxes and fast food like **burgers and fries**, costing between **¥600 and ¥1,200**. You can also leave the venue and eat at nearby cafes or ramen shops if you want a quieter spot.

After lunch, you can check out **panels** where game developers talk about upcoming games or meet them in person at **meet-and-greets**. If you're into game merchandise, there are booths selling **figures, posters, and limited edition items**, with prices ranging from **¥1,000 to ¥10,000**. When the day ends and you're ready to head back to Tokyo, trains run regularly from **Kaihin-Makuhari Station**, so it won't take long to get home.

8.2.2 ANIMEJAPAN

At **AnimeJapan**, held at **Tokyo Big Sight** in **Ariake, Tokyo**, you'll want to take the **Yurikamome Line** from **Shimbashi Station** or the **Rinkai Line** from **Osaki Station**. Both will bring you to stops that are around **5 to 10 minutes' walk** from the venue, either **Kokusai-Tenjijo Station** or **Tokyo Big Sight Station**. Arriving early is key, especially around **9:00 AM**, because the event officially starts at **10:00 AM** and the crowd builds up fast. It's smart to buy your tickets online to avoid long lines; prices are around **¥2,000 to ¥3,500** depending on the day.

Inside, you'll find huge halls packed with anime booths featuring franchises like **"Demon Slayer"** or **"Attack on Titan"**. Head straight to the booths you're most excited about to grab limited-edition merchandise because things sell out quickly. If you're interested in panels with **anime creators or voice actors**, be sure to get to the panel area in the **East Halls** at least **45 minutes early** to grab a seat, as they fill up fast.

If you're cosplaying, there are specific **changing rooms** and lockers that you can rent for about **¥500**, and the rules for cosplay are strict about prop sizes, so make sure your costume fits within guidelines. The **cosplay photo area** is where you'll find photographers snapping pics of all the creative outfits, and it's the perfect spot to show off your look. The food courts offer quick meals like **ramen, bento boxes, and takoyaki** that cost between **¥700 to ¥1,200**. It's a good idea to eat early, as lines build up around noon. For a break, head to the nearby **Ariake Garden** where you'll find cafes and restaurants with meals like **sushi** or **tempura**.

At the end of the day, if you don't want to deal with heavy crowds at **Tokyo Big Sight Station**, plan to leave before **5:00 PM**, since train stations will be packed. If you're staying in the **Odaiba** area, you'll have plenty of nearby restaurants for dinner, like **okonomiyaki spots** or ramen shops, with prices typically ranging from **¥1,500 to ¥2,500** for a meal.

8.2.3 KANDA MATSURI

The **Kanda Matsuri** happens around **Kanda Myojin Shrine** in **Chiyoda City**, and it's easy to get there by taking the **Tokyo Metro** to **Ochanomizu Station** or **Kanda Station**. From both stations, it's just a **5-10 minute walk** to the shrine. Public transport is busy but reliable during the festival, so you'll want to avoid driving as streets will be packed or closed. Walking from nearby areas like **Akihabara** or **Nihonbashi** is also a good option.

The main attraction is the **mikoshi**, the portable Shinto shrines carried through the streets. You'll find some of the best viewing spots on **Otemachi Avenue** or **Nihonbashi Street**, but you can also escape the largest crowds by heading to quieter spots near the **Kanda River** or **Suehirocho Station**. The festival really comes to life during the weekend before the third Sunday in May, with parades happening between **10 AM and 5 PM**, though getting there early gives you the best chance for a good view.

Food stalls will line the streets, offering things like **yakitori** for around **¥500-¥800**, **takoyaki** for **¥400-¥700**, and **okonomiyaki** for about **¥700-¥1,200**. For a sit-down meal, **Izuei Honten** is a 15-minute walk away at **1-6-1 Kanda Izumicho**, and you can try their famous **unagi** (eel dishes) starting at **¥1,800**. Another good spot nearby is **Sushizanmai Kanda East**, where sushi plates go for **¥150 to ¥2,000**, depending on what you order.

The festival has been around since the **Edo period**, originally celebrating the victory of the **Tokugawa shogunate**. Today, it's a celebration of prosperity and peace. At night, lanterns light up the streets as the **mikoshi** make their way back to the shrine, so stick around to see the final part of the parade. When you're ready to head home, stations like **Ochanomizu** and **Kanda** will be crowded, so it's best to leave a little earlier or hang around until the crowds thin out.

CHAPTER 9
UNIQUE ACCOMMODATIONS IN JAPAN

9.1 STAYING IN A RYOKAN

9.1.1 WHAT TO EXPECT

These traditional Japanese inns are most commonly found in scenic regions like **Kyoto, Hakone**, and **Nikko**, where you can enjoy the peaceful beauty of nature. In Kyoto, for example, you'll find ryokan near the historic **Gion** district, such as **Tawaraya Ryokan**, located on **Fuyacho Street**, a stone's throw away from **Kyoto Station**. To reach this particular area, you can easily hop on a **JR train** from Kyoto Station, which is well connected to Japan's national rail system, and take a short taxi ride or walk to the ryokan itself. In **Hakone**, ryokan such as **Gora Kadan** sit near the **Hakone-Yumoto Station**, a popular stop on the **Odakyu Line** from Shinjuku Station in Tokyo, and these spots offer unparalleled views of the mountains and hot spring baths.

Once you arrive at your ryokan, you'll be welcomed into a traditional **tatami-mat room**, where the simplicity of the layout creates an immediate sense of calm. After a day of exploring nearby attractions—whether it's the peaceful gardens of Kyoto or Hakone's open-air museums—you'll return to find your **futon bedding** laid out on the floor. Typically, a room attendant will arrange the futon in the evening, giving you a comfortable and minimalist sleeping space. The **futon** itself may be thin compared to Western beds, but it's surprisingly comfortable, often placed on soft tatami mats that add to the cozy atmosphere. Your room will be minimal yet elegant, with sliding **shoji** paper doors and possibly a **tokonoma** alcove where a simple flower arrangement or scroll serves as decoration.

At dinnertime, a **kaiseki meal** will likely be the highlight of your stay. Ryokan such as **Hiiragiya Ryokan** in Kyoto offer exquisite multi-course meals that focus on seasonal, local ingredients. These meals might include dishes such as fresh **sashimi**, seasonal **tempura**, and delicate **miso soup**, all beautifully arranged on fine porcelain. Expect to pay anywhere from **8,000 to 15,000 yen** for such meals, which are often included in your stay, though some high-end ryokan may charge separately. After dinner, you may want to relax in an **onsen** (hot spring bath). In places like Hakone, the natural geothermal activity provides piping-hot waters for the **onsen**, and many ryokan offer both indoor and outdoor baths. One ryokan with an incredible outdoor **onsen** is **Hakone Kowakien Ten-yu**, where you can bathe under the stars while overlooking lush forested hills. Just be sure to follow the onsen etiquette of washing thoroughly before entering the communal bath, and remember that **towels** should not be dipped in the water itself.

While staying at a ryokan, you'll be provided with a **yukata**, a casual cotton kimono that is comfortable to wear around the inn and even outside when strolling through the town. Ryokan like **Gion Hatanaka** in Kyoto encourage guests to wear their yukata as they explore the nearby **Yasaka Shrine** and traditional streets filled with quaint **tea houses** and local restaurants. To put on your yukata properly, make sure to fold the **left side over the right**, as folding it the opposite way is reserved for funerals. The yukata adds to the immersive traditional experience, and in cooler months, a **haori** (jacket) may also be provided.

For transport, **Hakone's ryokan** can be accessed from **Tokyo** via the **Odakyu Romancecar**—a scenic express train from **Shinjuku Station**—which takes about 90 minutes. Kyoto's ryokan are accessible via **Kyoto Station**, which connects to Tokyo through the **Tokaido Shinkansen**, a 2.5-hour ride. If you're traveling by public transport, many ryokan offer shuttle services from the nearest train station, or you can take a short taxi ride. **Ryokan stays** in popular regions typically range between **15,000 to 50,000 yen** per night, depending on the level of luxury and whether meals are included.

Nearby, you may find local attractions like **Higashiyama** in Kyoto or **Hakone's cable cars** and pirate ship cruises on **Lake Ashi**, offering stunning views of **Mount Fuji**. If you get hungry after a dip in the onsen, consider stopping by local eateries for **soba** or **tempura**, with some meals costing as little as **1,000 yen** in casual settings.

9.1.2 TOP RYOKAN DESTINATIONS

In Kyoto, you should stay at **Hiiragiya Ryokan** on **Shinmachi Street**. It's one of the oldest ryokan, and it's only a **10-minute walk from Karasuma Oike Station** on the **Kyoto Subway**. The rooms have **tatami-mat floors** and **futon beds** that are laid out for you in the evening. You can expect to pay around **40,000 yen** for a night here, which includes a traditional **kaiseki meal**. Near the ryokan, you can visit **Nishiki Market** for food and take a walk through **Gion**. If you want something cheaper to eat, you can stop by **Nishiki Warai**, where a meal costs about **2,000 yen**.

In **Hakone**, the best place to stay is **Gora Kadan** in **Gora**, a **5-minute walk from Gora Station**. It's famous for rooms with private **onsen (hot spring baths)**, with views of **Mount Fuji** or the surrounding nature. A night here is more expensive, starting at around **50,000 yen**. For something more budget-friendly, go for **Hakone Suimeisou Ryokan**, near **Hakone-Yumoto Station**, with prices starting from **15,000 yen per night**, and still offers a traditional ryokan experience with an onsen. While in **Hakone**, you can visit the **Hakone Open-Air Museum** or take a boat ride on **Lake Ashi**.

Nikko offers a more relaxed ryokan stay. You can try **Nikko Kanaya Hotel**, near **Toshogu Shrine**, a **UNESCO World Heritage Site**. It's just a **10-minute bus ride from Nikko Station** and costs around **20,000 yen per night**. Close by, you can enjoy **Lake Chuzenji** and **Kegon Falls**. For food, check out **Kikko-en** for a traditional **yuba (tofu skin)** meal, costing around **1,500 yen**. For a coastal option, head to the **Izu Peninsula** and stay at **Arcana Izu** along the **Kawazu River**. It's quiet and offers private onsens with river views. Rooms cost about **30,000 yen per night**, and it's near **Shuzenji Station**. You can visit the **Shuzenji Temple** and nearby **Bamboo Forest Path**. If you're hungry, go to **Isokaze** near **Izu Kogen Station** for **sashimi bowls**, costing between **1,200 and 2,500 yen**.

9.2 CAPSULE HOTELS

9.2.1 HOW CAPSULE HOTELS WORK

staying at a capsule hotel, like **Nine Hours Shinjuku-North**, you'll find it just a **5-minute walk from JR Shinjuku Station**, right on **Okubo Street**, making it easy to reach if you're coming from Narita or Haneda airports. Just hop on the Narita Express or the Tokyo Monorail to Shinjuku Station, and you'll be there in no time. **Nine Hours** is located in a busy part of Shinjuku, with tons of shopping, restaurants, and entertainment nearby. It costs around **4,500 yen per night**, making it affordable. Close by, you can grab a bowl of **Ichiran Ramen** on **Kabu-kicho Street** for about **890 yen**. It's perfect for a quick, late-night meal after exploring.

If you're in Osaka, **First Cabin Midosuji Namba** is a great choice. It's just a **3-minute walk from Namba Station**, so you can get there easily if you're coming from the airport or using the Shinkansen to **Shin-Osaka Station**. Staying here costs around **4,500 to 6,000 yen per night**. From here, you're just **10 minutes on foot to Dotonbori Street**, where you can try **takoyaki** or **okonomiyaki** and check out the lively nightlife. Both Tokyo and Osaka capsule hotels have shared showers, lockers, and some common spaces where you can relax or plan your next day.

9.2.2 CAPSULE HOTEL ETIQUETTE

In a capsule hotel, everything is designed for space-saving and convenience. You'll sleep in a small, pod-like room that's just big enough for a bed, but it's clean and modern, with some privacy thanks to sliding doors or curtains. Facilities like bathrooms and showers are shared, and there are lockers for your personal items. Many capsule hotels, especially in places like **Tokyo** (Shinjuku, Shibuya) or **Osaka** (Namba, Dotonbori), are close to train stations, making it easy to get around. For example, in **Shinjuku**, you can stay at **Nine Hours Shinjuku North**, just a short walk from **Shinjuku Station**, which connects to the **JR**

Yamanote Line. In **Osaka**, **Capsule Hotel Astil Dotonbori** is near **Namba Station** on the **Midosuji Line**, perfect for exploring the city.

Prices for a night in a capsule hotel range from **3,500 yen to 6,000 yen**, depending on the location. You'll check in around **3 p.m.** and check out by **10 a.m.**, though some offer day-use rates if you need a quick nap. It's easy to reach these hotels from the airports—**Narita Express** takes you from **Narita Airport** to **Shinjuku** in about **90 minutes for 3,000 yen**, and in Osaka, the **Nankai Airport Line** gets you from **Kansai International Airport** to **Namba** in about **45 minutes for 920 yen**.

While staying, it's important to keep quiet, especially at night, because sound can travel between capsules. **Lockers** are provided to keep the sleeping area tidy, and some hotels offer **women-only floors** for added privacy. You'll find some hotels that provide **pajamas and toiletries**, but it's a good idea to bring your own just in case. **Food options** are usually nearby; in **Shinjuku**, you're close to the famous **Omoide Yokocho** alley with tiny bars and restaurants, while in **Namba**, you can walk down **Dotonbori** and try dishes like **takoyaki** or **okonomiyaki** for about **600 to 1,000 yen**

9.3 TEMPLE LODGING

9.3.1 STAYING IN A SHUKUBO

When you stay at a **shukubo** (temple lodging) in **Mount Koya**, you'll experience living alongside monks and getting a glimpse into their quiet, spiritual life. To get to **Mount Koya**, take the **Nankai Koya Line** from **Namba Station** in Osaka, which takes about two hours. Once you reach **Gokurakubashi Station**, you'll transfer to a cable car that takes you up to **Koyasan Station**, and from there, local buses will bring you to the different temples where you can stay. The bus ride from the station costs about **420 yen**.

You'll find rooms with **tatami mats** and **futon bedding** that the staff will set up in the evening. A typical night at a **shukubo** costs between **10,000 and 20,000 yen**, and it usually includes meals. Expect **shojin ryori**, a simple, vegetarian meal made with fresh ingredients like tofu, vegetables, and miso. You'll also have access to the temple's peaceful grounds, and can even participate in activities like **Zen meditation** or join the monks for **morning prayers**, where you can sit quietly and listen to their chanting.

Most of the temples are located near **Koya Dori** and **Okunoin Dori**, close to the famous **Okunoin Cemetery** and **Danjo Garan** temple complex. These are must-see spots while you're here. The temples offer a tranquil experience, so expect quiet surroundings. If you're planning to eat outside the temple, check out small cafes along **Koya Dori**, where you can get a simple dish like **udon** or **soba** noodles for **500 to 1,000 yen**.

I suggest you to book in advance, especially during busy times like **New Year's** or **Obon**. You can do this through the **Koyasan Shukubo Association** or directly on the temple websites. Bring warm clothes, as it can get cool in the mornings and evenings.

9.3.2 TOP TEMPLE LODGINGS

To get to **Mount Koya**, you can take the **Nankai Koya Line** from **Namba Station** in Osaka, which will get you to **Gokurakubashi Station** in about **1 hour and 30 minutes**. From there, you'll hop on the **Koya Cable Car**, which takes you up to the top of the mountain. Once you arrive, there are buses that stop at many of the **temples** offering lodging. Two popular temple stays are **Eko-in** and **Fukuchi-in**, where you'll sleep in **tatami rooms**, eat traditional **vegetarian meals**, and take part in **Zen meditation sessions**. Staying at a temple usually costs between **10,000 and 20,000 yen per night**, depending on what's included.

While at Mount Koya, you can visit **Okunoin Cemetery**, the largest cemetery in Japan, where you'll find **ancient cedar trees** and **thousands of gravestones**, creating a peaceful environment. The **Danjo Garan Temple Complex** nearby is also worth seeing, with its impressive **Konpon Daito Pagoda**. You can grab something to eat nearby at small restaurants like **Bon On Shya** on **Koyasan Street**, where a simple meal costs around **1,200 yen**.

In **Nagano**, another great option for temple lodging is **Zenko-ji Temple**, located about **15 minutes** from **Nagano Station** by bus. The stay includes joining the **morning Buddhist prayers**, and it's priced between **7,000 and 15,000 yen**. You can reach **Nagano Station** from **Tokyo** via the **Shinkansen**, which takes about **1 hour 30 minutes**. When you stay here, you'll also have a chance to visit **Togakushi Shrine** or see the famous **snow monkeys** at **Jigokudani Monkey Park**. Then, If you want something even quieter, try **Hida Koyasan Temple**, near **Takayama**. It's about a **30-minute bus ride** from **Takayama Station** and offers a peaceful stay in the **Hida mountains**, with prices ranging from **8,000 to 12,000 yen** per night. While you're there, you can explore the **Hida Folk Village** to see old traditional houses, or grab a meal of **Hida beef** at **Kotte Ushi** on **Honmachi Street**, where a set meal starts around **2,500 yen**.

9.4 GLAMPING AND LUXURY STAYS

9.4.1 BEST GLAMPING SITES

One of the top places to go is **Hoshinoya Fuji** near **Mount Fuji**. It's located in **Fujikawaguchiko**, and you can get there by taking the **Chuo Highway Bus** from **Shinjuku Station** in **Tokyo** to **Kawaguchiko Station**. The bus ride takes about **2 hours and 30 minutes**, and then it's a quick **10-minute** taxi or shuttle ride to the glamping site. Prices start around **35,000 yen per night**, depending on the season. You'll have a cozy tent with a real bed, private bathroom, and amazing views of **Mount Fuji**. The best time to go is spring for cherry blossoms or autumn for clear skies and cool weather. Nearby, you can go for a walk by the lake, try canoeing, or enjoy stargazing at night. Don't miss out on trying **Hoto noodles** from local restaurants, a specialty in the area.

In **Hokkaido**, a great spot for glamping is **The Lodge Makkari**, located in **Makkari Village** near **Niseko**. You can get there by taking a bus from **Sapporo Station** to **Kutchan**, which takes about **45 minutes**. Prices here start around **20,000 yen per night**, and the tents are heated, which is great because **Hokkaido** can get chilly even in summer. It's a perfect place if you love hiking or skiing, and after a day of exploring, you can relax at **Makkari Onsen**. If you're hungry, you can enjoy fresh seafood from the local restaurants in **Niseko Village**, just a short drive away.

For a beachside glamping experience, head to **GlampOkinawa** in **Nanjo**, **Okinawa**. It's located at **Tamagusuku Maekawa**, and you can get there by taking a **45-minute** bus ride from **Naha Airport**. The tents are right by the ocean, and prices start around **40,000 yen per night**. You'll have private showers, air conditioning, and amazing sea views. You can spend your time snorkeling or swimming, and there are food stalls nearby where you can try fresh seafood and **taco rice**. If you're into history, **Sefa Utaki**, a sacred site, is close by, and it's definitely worth a visit.

9.4.2 LUXURY HOTELS AND RESORTS

For true luxury in **Tokyo**, start with the renowned **Aman Tokyo** located inside **Otemachi Tower** at **1-5-6 Otemachi, Chiyoda City**. This hotel offers a minimalist yet luxurious Japanese experience, and it's incredibly convenient to reach, just a **5-minute walk** from **Otemachi Station** on the **Tokyo Metro** lines, which makes it easy to explore nearby attractions like the **Imperial Palace Gardens** and the business districts around **Marunouchi**. Rooms here start at around **100,000 yen per night**, and you'll find spacious accommodations with panoramic views of the city skyline, along with private onsen baths that offer the perfect blend of relaxation and city life. Dining in-house at **The Restaurant by Aman** allows you to indulge in Michelin-level cuisine, with meals ranging from **10,000 yen to 20,000 yen**, making it an unforgettable high-end dining experience.

In **Kyoto**, look no further than **The Ritz-Carlton Kyoto** located at **Kamogawa Nijo-Ohashi, Nakagyo Ward**, right along the scenic **Kamogawa River**. This luxurious property offers stunning views of the **Higashiyama Mountains**, and you can reach it in about **15 minutes** on foot from **Gion-Shijo Station** on the **Keihan Line**. Rooms here start at approximately **90,000 yen per night**, and the hotel's location makes it ideal for exploring **Gion**, **Pontocho**, and the many temples and shrines nearby, such as the iconic **Kiyomizu-dera** and **Yasaka Shrine**. Guests can enjoy cultural activities like private tea ceremonies or hire a guide to tour **Kyoto's famous temples**. For food lovers, try **Mizuki**, the hotel's on-site restaurant offering kaiseki meals at around **15,000 yen per person**, or explore nearby eateries like **Gion Maruyama**, where you can taste traditional Kyoto kaiseki meals in an authentic setting for around **12,000 to 20,000 yen**.

Gora Kadan in **Hakone**, located at **1300 Gora, Hakone**, is a perfect retreat. It's a short **5-minute walk from Gora Station** on the **Hakone Tozan Line**, making it easy to visit nearby attractions such as the **Hakone Open-Air Museum** and **Hakone Gora Park**. Prices here start at **70,000 yen per night**, but what truly sets it apart is the chance to experience a traditional ryokan stay with luxury touches —think private onsen baths, multi-course kaiseki meals served in-room, and the beauty of the mountains surrounding you. After a day of soaking in hot springs or hiking trails like **Owakudani** and **Lake Ashi**, relax with a meal at **Sushimasa**, located nearby at **3-13-1 Gora**, where you can enjoy high-quality sushi for around **5,000 yen**.

For a tropical beach, **The Ritz-Carlton Okinawa** is situated in **Nago** at **1343-1 Kise, Nago, Okinawa**, about a **90-minute drive from Naha Airport**. The resort offers private beaches and ocean views, with luxurious rooms starting around **80,000 yen per night**. Nearby, you can enjoy Okinawa's famous coral reefs and pristine beaches, with activities like snorkeling, diving, and beach yoga, while the on-site restaurants, such as **Kise**, serve fresh local seafood dishes for around **7,000 yen** per person. The hotel is close to **Busena Marine Park** and **Manza Beach**, making it easy to explore both natural and cultural landmarks while indulging in five-star luxury. Public transport isn't as frequent in Okinawa as in Tokyo or Kyoto, so renting a car is recommended for getting around and visiting nearby attractions.

CHAPTER 10
ULTIMATE PRACTICAL PLANNING GUIDE

10.1 BUDGETING FOR JAPAN

10.1.1 ESTIMATING YOUR TRIP COST

For your Japan trip, **flight prices** will be your first big expense, and they change based on the time of year and where you're flying from. Flights usually range from **$700 to $1,500** depending on the season, with prices higher in spring and fall, especially during **cherry blossom season** in April or **autumn foliage** in November. When it comes to **accommodation**, you'll find everything from cheap **capsule hotels** that cost about **¥3,000 to ¥5,000 per night**, all the way to luxurious **ryokan** with private hot springs and gourmet meals that can go up to **¥50,000 per night** or more. In areas like **Kyoto, Hakone,** or **Nikko,** the higher-end ryokan offer stunning views, incredible hospitality, and peaceful settings, but even the budget options give you a taste of traditional Japanese hospitality without breaking the bank.

You can eat really well even if you're watching your budget. A quick meal of **ramen, gyudon,** or a **bento** box from a convenience store will cost you about **¥1,000 per meal**, while a more traditional and elaborate dining experience, like a multi-course **kaiseki** dinner at a nice restaurant, will be a lot pricier—around **¥10,000 or more per person**. If you're planning to visit temples, shrines, and cultural sites, the entry fees are quite low, averaging **¥500 to ¥1,000** per site. These fees might not seem like much, but if you're visiting multiple temples in places like **Kyoto**, they can add up quickly. **Transportation** is another major cost to consider, and the **7-day JR Pass** for **¥29,650** is a good deal if you're traveling between cities like **Tokyo, Kyoto**, and **Osaka**, as it gives you unlimited travel on the **Shinkansen** and other JR trains. However, for shorter trips or regional travel, you might find cheaper alternatives like local day passes.

One important thing to remember is that **tipping isn't necessary** in Japan — in fact, it's not even customary. You won't need to tip at restaurants, hotels, or taxis, so you don't have to worry about that. Some higher-end places might include a small **service charge** in the bill, but otherwise, you're good to go. As for **money**, cash is still widely used, especially in smaller shops and restaurants, so it's smart to carry both cash and cards. **ATMs in 7-Eleven stores** are the most reliable for withdrawing money with foreign cards, and you'll find these convenience stores all over the country. You have to make sure you have enough local currency, especially when you travel outside of the bigger cities, where **cash-only** establishments are more common.

10.1.2 MONEY-SAVING TIPS

Visiting multiple cities, consider the **JR Pass**, which is particularly useful for long-distance journeys—if you're traveling between major destinations like **Tokyo, Kyoto**, and **Osaka**, a **7-day JR Pass** costing **¥29,650** will likely save you a significant amount compared to purchasing individual tickets, especially if you plan to take the **Shinkansen**. If you're focusing on a specific region, options like the **Kansai Area Pass** for travel within **Kyoto, Osaka**, and surrounding areas can offer even better value, allowing you unlimited train access for a set period without overspending.

When it comes to attractions, you'll find that many of the most iconic sites don't require an entry fee at all. For example, you can enjoy the peaceful atmosphere of **Meiji Shrine** in **Tokyo** or explore the famous **Fushimi Inari Shrine** in **Kyoto**, both completely free. You can spend hours wandering through these historical and cultural sites without touching your wallet. Additionally, public parks like **Yoyogi Park** or **Shinjuku Gyoen** in **Tokyo**, or the beautiful **Arashiyama Bamboo Grove** in **Kyoto**, provide tranquil spots where you can enjoy nature without paying an entrance fee, making these great options for budget-conscious travelers. Visiting during festivals like the **Gion Matsuri** or the **Sumida River Fireworks Festival** offers a unique cultural experience at no cost, allowing you to witness the energy of Japan's traditional celebrations.

For accommodation, you can stay in **hostels, capsule hotels**, or budget-friendly **Airbnb** options, with nightly rates ranging from **¥2,000 to ¥4,000**, depending on your location and time of travel. These affordable options are plentiful in major cities like **Tokyo** and **Osaka**, and they offer clean, modern spaces to sleep, often equipped with free Wi-Fi and shared kitchens. If you're staying longer or moving around the country, it's worth checking out guesthouses that provide a more communal experience and are usually cheaper than hotels.

Dining on a budget is easy if you head to **supermarkets** and **convenience stores** like **7-Eleven**, **Lawson**, or **FamilyMart**, which offer prepared meals such as **onigiri (rice balls)**, **bento boxes**, or **soba noodles** that you can grab for less than **¥500**. These stores are everywhere, from the heart of **Shibuya** in **Tokyo** to smaller towns, and you can rely on them for a quick, inexpensive meal. Alternatively, if you prefer a sit-down experience without breaking the bank, head to family restaurants like **Saizeriya** or **Gusto**, which serve satisfying meals for under **¥1,000**.

To save even more, use apps like **Klook** or **Voyagin**, which offer discounted tickets for attractions and activities—whether you're looking for deals on **museums**, **guided tours**, or even **amusement parks**, these platforms frequently offer promotions that can help you stretch your budget further. You can find discounts on popular spots like **Tokyo Skytree**, **Universal Studios Japan**, or even **DisneySea** in **Chiba**, and they often feature promotions for limited-time cultural events.

10.2 HOW TO USE THE JR PASS

10.2.1 JR PASS

The **JR Pass** is perfect if you plan to travel between cities. You can choose between **7 days for ¥29,650, 14 days for ¥47,250, or 21 days for ¥60,450**. This pass gives you **unlimited rides** on almost all JR trains, including the **Shinkansen (bullet trains)**, but not the fastest ones (Nozomi and Mizuho). The other Shinkansen options, like **Hikari**, are still fast and get you to places like **Tokyo, Kyoto, Osaka**, and **Hiroshima** easily. You need to **buy the pass before you come to the country**. You can get it online or through an agent, and when you arrive, you'll exchange it for the real pass at **major JR stations or airports** like **Narita, Haneda, or Kansai**. You'll pick a start date, and it'll work for **consecutive days** from that date. Be sure to plan your first use carefully because the countdown starts once it's activated.

With the JR Pass, you can travel on **JR trains, some buses, and even ferries**, like the ferry to **Miyajima Island** near Hiroshima. To use it, you just show it at the **manned gates** at JR stations. It's best for long trips. For example, a round trip between **Tokyo and Kyoto** on the Shinkansen would normally cost you around ¥28,000, so the pass quickly pays for itself if you're traveling a lot.

In **Tokyo**, the pass covers the **JR Yamanote Line**, which is great for getting to popular places like **Shibuya, Shinjuku, Akihabara**, and **Ueno**. If you're in **Kyoto**, it covers the **JR Sagano Line**, which takes you to **Arashiyama** for the **bamboo forest**.

You can also use the JR Pass to visit places like **Nikko** by taking the **Tobu-Nikko Line** from **Shinjuku Station** to see the **Toshogu Shrine**. In **Hokkaido**, you can use the pass on JR-operated buses to get around more rural areas.

You can **reserve seats** for free with your pass, which is great if you're traveling during busy times, like **Golden Week** or holidays. You just go to a **JR ticket office** to reserve your seat. Just remember, it doesn't work on non-JR subways or private rail lines, so in cities like **Tokyo** or **Osaka**, you might need an **IC card** like **Suica** or **Pasmo** for other transport. But for long distances or JR lines, it's a huge money saver.

For food, in places like **Miyajima**, try local dishes like grilled oysters for around ¥300, or sweet **Momiji-manju** for about ¥100. You'll find these near popular spots like the **Itsukushima Shrine**.

The JR Pass also works on the **Narita Express** from **Narita Airport** and the **Haruka Express** from **Kansai Airport**, making it easy to get into the city right after your flight.

TIPS

When you use your **JR Pass**, start by making **seat reservations** for your Shinkansen trips. You do this at any **JR ticket office (Midori no Madoguchi)** inside the larger train stations. It's simple: tell the staff where you're going and when, and they'll find you the best train. During busy travel seasons like **Golden Week** or the **New Year holidays**, reservations are essential to guarantee you a seat, even though some trains have non-reserved seating, but getting a seat is key to a comfortable trip.

For city travel, your **JR Pass** works on local JR lines. In **Tokyo**, you'll use it on the **Yamanote Line**, which loops through major neighborhoods like **Shibuya**, **Harajuku**, and **Shinjuku**. This line connects to most of the city's top attractions, and you'll be able to use the pass as many times as you like. In **Osaka**, the **JR Osaka Loop Line** works the same way, taking you around the city, to places like **Osaka Castle** and **Universal Studios Japan**, so you won't need any extra tickets for JR trains within the city.

Your pass even works on the **JR ferry to Miyajima Island** from **Miya-jimaguchi Station**, where you can see the famous **floating torii gate** at Itsukushima Shrine. This is one of the best ways to use your pass because the ferry ride itself offers fantastic views, and the shrine is a must-see on your trip.

You should definitely use **apps like Hyperdia** for planning. Hyperdia will let you see **all train schedules** and help you avoid trains not covered by the pass. Just enter your destination, and you'll get all the info: times, connections, and which platform to head to. It's easy and makes traveling stress-free. **Google Maps** also works well for local navigation and walking directions between stations or to plan how to get from one place to another without getting lost.

If you're sticking to one region, like **Kanto (Tokyo area)** or **Kansai (Osaka, Kyoto)**, consider a **regional JR Pass** instead of the national one. The **JR East Pass** is perfect if you're exploring Tokyo and nearby places like **Nikko** or **Hakone**, and the **JR West Pass** is great for Osaka, Kyoto, and Nara. These regional passes are cheaper and still give you all the benefits of seat reservations and unlimited travel within their areas, so if you're not moving all over the country, it's the smarter choice.

10.3 APPS

10.3.1 SUGGEST TRAVEL APPS

You'll want to start with **Hyperdia** to plan all your train trips. It's perfect for checking **real-time train schedules, platform numbers, and connections.** If you're heading from **Tokyo Station** to **Kyoto Station**, for example, you just enter the stations, and Hyperdia will show you the next available Shinkansen, including which platform to go to and how long the journey will take—usually about 2 hours and 30 minutes on the **Hikari Shinkansen**. You'll also see if you need to make any transfers along the way. It's especially useful with your **JR Pass** because it filters out any trains not covered by the pass, like the **Nozomi Shinkansen**, which isn't included. Make sure to use it for long trips, like traveling from **Shinjuku Station** in Tokyo to **Osaka**, or even shorter routes like **Nagoya to Takayama**. Trains usually run every 10-20 minutes, but the app will give you exact times and allow you to plan transfers easily.

For getting around cities, **Google Maps** is your go-to. If you're in **Tokyo**, for instance, and want to visit **Asakusa** from **Shibuya**, it'll show you which subway lines to take (probably the **Ginza Line** from **Shibuya Station**). The app gives you walking directions too, so if you're walking around **Shibuya Crossing** and want to head to **Harajuku** for shopping on **Takeshita Street**, you'll know exactly how long the walk will be and where to turn. It's also really helpful for figuring out public transport timings, as it shows exact train and bus schedules, and it'll even suggest faster routes if traffic or delays pop up. Use it in places like **Kyoto**, where you can plan a route from **Kyoto Station** to **Kinkaku-ji** by bus or train, knowing exactly when the bus leaves and how long the ride will take (usually around 40 minutes by bus).

To stay connected with locals, download **LINE**. In Japan, everyone uses LINE to chat and make calls, and you'll find it helpful for communicating with your **Airbnb host** or if you're making a **restaurant reservation**. If you're staying in **Shibuya** and booking a table at a popular place like **Uobei Sushi** (a conveyor belt sushi spot on **Dogenzaka Street**), the restaurant might ask you to confirm via LINE. It's also great for meeting up with other travelers or getting local tips on where to eat or what to do.

For language help, as you may know already the app **Google Translate** will save you in situations where English isn't common, like in smaller towns or traditional restaurants. If you're in **Kyoto** and sitting down for dinner in **Pontocho Alley** (where menus are often written only in Japanese), just snap a picture of the menu, and Google Translate will give you a rough idea of what's on offer. It's also super useful if you're traveling in the countryside, like in **Takayama** or **Nara**, where fewer people speak English. You can also use the voice function to have quick conversations with shopkeepers or taxi drivers—just speak your question into the app, and it will translate it immediately.

If you're feeling too tired after a day of sightseeing, use **Uber Eats** to get food delivered to your hotel or Airbnb. In **Tokyo**, you can order food from local places or international chains, whether you want sushi from a place near **Roppongi Hills** or ramen from a shop in **Shinjuku**. Delivery fees vary, usually around ¥200-¥500, and meals can range from ¥1,000-¥2,000, depending on what you order. It's a convenient option if you've spent the whole day exploring **Tsukiji Market** or **Akihabara** and just want to relax back at your place.

10.3.2 HOW TO ACCESS FREE WI-FI AND DATA PLANS

You'll find **free Wi-Fi** in places like **Starbucks**, **Doutor**, and many train stations, like **Tokyo Station** or **Shibuya Station**. Just connect with your **email**. At **Narita** or **Haneda Airport**, free Wi-Fi is available right after you land. It's good for checking maps or quick searches, but it can be slow during busy times.

For full internet access wherever you go, rent a **portable Wi-Fi device**. Pick one up at **Narita**, **Haneda**, or **Kansai Airport** from companies like **Japan Wireless** or **Ninja Wi-Fi**. They usually cost around **¥500 to ¥1,000 per day**. You can connect multiple devices, and it works everywhere, whether you're in **Shibuya** or out in the **Hakone mountains**. Reserve it online before your trip and pick it up when you land. Return it at the airport before you leave.

If you want to use your phone, get a **SIM card**. Buy one at **Bic Camera** or **Yodobashi Camera** near places like **Shinjuku Station** or **Akihabara**, or right at the airport. SIM cards start at **¥2,000** for a **7-day plan** with about **3GB of data**. If you need more data for streaming or maps, go for an unlimited plan, which costs around **¥4,500** for 30 days. Just make sure your phone is **unlocked** before you arrive, or it won't work.

When using **public Wi-Fi**, especially in busy places like **Shibuya** or **Osaka Station**, use a **VPN** to protect your personal data. It keeps your information safe when you're connected to open networks.

If you're out exploring, stay connected to find great restaurants. For example, in **Asakusa**, try **Tempura Tendon Tenya** near **Asakusa Station** for a meal under ¥1,000. Or in **Shibuya**, visit **Ichiran Ramen** on **Dogenzaka Street** for about ¥900. You can use your internet connection to check reviews or book tables using **LINE**, the local messaging app.

Returning the **portable Wi-Fi** is easy. Drop it off at the airport or mail it back before you leave. If you used a **SIM card**, just remove it once your plan is over.

10.4 PACKING TIPS BY SEASON

10.4.1 SPRING AND SUMMER

In **spring**, when the weather changes a lot between **10°C to 20°C**, you'll want to pack **light layers**. Mornings and evenings can still feel chilly, especially if you're out enjoying **hanami** in spots like **Ueno Park** or walking along the **Kamo River** in **Kyoto**. Bring a **light jacket or sweater** that you can easily take off as it warms up during the day. The cherry blossoms make everything look magical, but you need to stay warm early in the morning or after the sun goes down. You can add or remove layers as the temperature changes.

By **summer**—especially **June through August**—the heat and humidity will hit hard, especially in **Kyoto** or **Tokyo**, where it gets over **30°C**. You need **breathable fabrics** like **cotton** or **linen**. **Loose-fitting clothes** are your best bet since tight clothes will feel uncomfortable with the humidity. You'll want a **hat**, **sunglasses**, and definitely **sunscreen** if you're visiting places like **Fushimi Inari Shrine** or walking through **Osaka** all day. The sun is strong, and you'll feel it, especially during long outdoor trips. Even if you're just walking between shops in **Ginza** or checking out the food stalls at **Nishiki Market**, it's easy to get overheated, so plan your outfits around staying cool.

Starting in **June**, the **rainy season** lasts until mid-July, so you need to be ready for **heavy rains** that come on suddenly. Always carry a **foldable umbrella** or a **compact raincoat** with you. A good raincoat that packs small is perfect because you can throw it on quickly when those downpours start. You don't want to be stuck in the rain in **Shinjuku** or while hiking in **Nikko** without one, especially since it can rain heavily for hours. It's also a good idea to wear **quick-drying shoes** or **sandals**, as streets can flood easily during sudden showers, and wet shoes will make your day pretty uncomfortable.

If you're heading to one of the many **summer festivals**, like **Gion Matsuri** in **Kyoto**, consider wearing a **yukata**. They are lightweight cotton kimonos that are perfect for the hot, sticky nights of the summer festivals, and they let you blend in with the locals. You can find yukatas for sale in places like **Asakusa** or **Kyoto's Gion district** for around **¥3,000 to ¥5,000**, and they come with everything you need, including the **obi** and **geta** (sandals). Wearing one adds to the festival experience, whether you're watching the **Gion Matsuri parade** or dancing at **Awa Odori** in **Tokushima**.

Don't forget about **comfortable walking shoes**. You'll be walking a lot, whether you're visiting temples in **Kyoto**, exploring **Nara Park**, or strolling through the streets of **Osaka**. Make sure your shoes are broken in before you go. If you're hiking, like in **Arashiyama** or the **Fuji Five Lakes** area, supportive shoes are essential, as the uneven terrain can be tough on your feet.

10.4.2 AUTUMN AND WINTER

For **autumn**, as temperatures drop to **10°C to 15°C** between **September and November**, you'll need **warm layers** to stay comfortable throughout the day. In places like **Kyoto** or **Nikko**, the mornings and evenings can be quite chilly, so make sure to pack a **light sweater** or **fleece** that you can wear with a **jacket**. This is especially important when you're walking through parks to see the fall colors or visiting outdoor temples. You'll be outside a lot, and the air feels cooler near rivers or in the mountains, so a **scarf** helps too. It's all about layers—you can add or remove them as the temperature changes throughout the day, especially since the afternoons might still feel warm under the sun.

By the time **winter** arrives, especially between **December and February**, the cold becomes much more intense, especially if you're headed to places like **Hokkaido** or the **Japanese Alps**, where temperatures can drop to **-10°C** or lower. In these regions, you'll need a **thick insulated jacket** to handle the cold, along with **thermal layers**. Make sure you pack **thermal leggings** and **wool socks**— these will help you stay warm whether you're skiing in **Niseko** or just walking around snowy streets. In cities like **Tokyo** and **Osaka**, winter is less extreme, but you'll still need a **warm coat**, especially for the colder evenings. You'll want to be comfortable when exploring outdoor markets or watching **light displays** during the winter months. **Gloves** and a **hat** are important too, even in the city, as the wind can make it feel much colder than the actual temperature.

For **traveling light**, pack compact but warm essentials like **thermal underwear** and **wool sweaters**. These items don't take up much space but are key to keeping warm. A **packable down jacket** is also great, as it provides warmth without bulk and can fit easily into your bag. **Wool socks** are useful not just for warmth but because they dry quickly, which is handy if your feet get wet while walking in rain or snow.

If you're planning an **onsen** visit during your trip, especially in colder regions like **Hakone** or **Kinosaki Onsen**, it's smart to bring a **small towel** for washing before you enter the baths. Most onsen provide large towels for drying off and

yukata for you to wear after the bath, but having your own small towel makes the process easier. Also, remember to pack **comfortable slippers**. Many onsen require you to take off your shoes before entering, and slippers make it easier to walk around the bathhouse or inn. For outdoor onsen, like those in **Hakone**, where you have to walk outside briefly to get to the baths, wearing something warm after your soak—like a **scarf or jacket**—will help you stay comfortable in the cold air.

CHAPTER 11
ESSENTIAL JAPANESE PHRASES AND LANGUAGE TIPS

12.1 BASIC JAPANESE PHRASES FOR TRAVELERS

12.1.1 COMMON GREETINGS AND PHRASES

When you're out and about, you'll need to know a few key phrases to help you get around and interact with people. Start with **Konnichiwa**, which is the word for **hello**. You can use this during the day in places like shops or when you're asking someone for help. If it's early in the morning, say **Ohayou gozaimasu** instead, which means **good morning**. You'll hear locals say **Ohayou** casually, but adding **gozaimasu** makes it polite enough for anyone.

When you want to thank someone, say **Arigato gozaimasu**. Use it after someone gives you directions, helps you, or serves you in a restaurant. If it's a more relaxed setting, like when you're hanging out with friends or people your age, just say **Arigato**. If someone does something extra nice for you, say **Domo arigato gozaimasu** to show extra gratitude.

To get someone's attention, like a waiter or when you're asking for help, say **Sumimasen**. You'll use it a lot, whether you're trying to pass through a crowded place or calling over staff in a restaurant. If you're walking around busy streets, like **Shibuya Crossing**, or asking for the bill in a café, **Sumimasen** works well to get the message across politely.

For asking directions, use **Doko desu ka?**, which means **where is....** If you're looking for the bathroom, say **Toire wa doko desu ka?**. If you're trying to find a train station, say **Eki wa doko desu ka?**. This is a simple, useful phrase you can combine with almost any place you're trying to find.

When you're ready to pay in a restaurant, say **Okaikei onegaishimasu**, which means **the bill, please**. Whether you're eating at a ramen shop or a small café, this phrase works and will help you get the check without any confusion.

Always use polite forms like **Arigato gozaimasu** and **Sumimasen** when talking to people you don't know.

12.1.2 IMPORTANT PHRASES FOR TRANSPORT

When you're buying a train or bus ticket, just say **Kippu o kudasai**, which means **a ticket, please**. If you're going to a specific place, like **Tokyo Station**, make it clearer by saying **Tokyo eki made no kippu o kudasai**, which means **a ticket to Tokyo Station, please**. You'll use this at busy spots like **Shinjuku Station** or **Kyoto Station**, especially when the ticket machines are crowded, and you need to ask at the counter. It's good to know this phrase when you're traveling to smaller towns where English isn't always available at the machine, like in **Nikko** or **Hakone**.

When you're inside a big station, it can get confusing quickly. If you're looking for an entrance, you need to follow the signs that say **iriguchi** for **entrance**, and for exits, look for **deguchi**. When you're trying to find your platform, follow the signs that say **noriba**, which means **platform**. But if you're lost, you can ask, **Noriba wa doko desu ka?**, which means **where is the platform?** This is especially important in huge, complex stations like **Shibuya** or **Osaka**, where it's easy to take a wrong turn and end up at the wrong platform.

If you're worried about your train or bus being late, or if you want to double-check the schedule, you can ask **Kono densha wa jikan doori desu ka?**, which means **is this train on time?**. When you want to know when the next one is leaving, just say **Jikan o oshiete kudasai**, which is how you ask someone to **tell you the time** for the next train or bus. This will be helpful when you're catching a bullet train or taking long trips between cities, like from **Tokyo to Kyoto**, where being on time is really important.

Taking a **taxi** is easy if you know how to say the name of your destination followed by **made onegaishimasu**, which means **to this place, please**. So, if you want to go to **Shibuya Station**, you'll say **Shibuya eki made onegaishimasu**. This is useful in busy areas like **Roppongi** or **Shinjuku**, where traffic is fast, and you need to communicate quickly and clearly. If you're unsure the driver understands, politely ask **Wakarimasu ka?**, which means **do you understand?** It's the best way to make sure there's no confusion, especially if you're going somewhere less known or outside the city center. Taxi fares usually start around ¥700, and it's good to have enough cash on hand just in case, especially if you're outside the main cities.

On a bus or train, when you're not sure if it's your stop, or you didn't catch the announcement, just say **Sumimasen, mou ichido onegaishimasu**, which means **excuse me, could you repeat that?** This works when you're not sure about which stop is coming next, especially when there aren't many signs in English, like in rural areas or on less crowded routes, such as buses in **Takayama** or **Nara**.

If you need to ask where the **ticket counter** is, you'll say **Kippu no uriba wa doko desu ka?**, which means **where is the ticket counter?** This will help you find your way in bigger stations like **Narita Airport** or **Tokyo Station**, where it's easy to get lost with all the levels and exits.

12.2 HOW TO COMMUNICATE EFFECTIVELY WITHOUT SPEAKING JAPANESE

12.2.1 USING TECHNOLOGY TO BRIDGE THE LANGUAGE GAP

When you don't speak the language, **voice translation apps** are the easiest way to communicate. Use **Google Translate** or **iTranslate**—just speak into your phone, and the app will translate what you're saying into Japanese. If you're in a **restaurant** on **Omotesando Street** in **Shibuya**, and you need to order food, the app can help you explain your dietary needs or ask about the menu. You can do the same in a **shop** like **Don Quijote** to ask for a specific item, or at a **train station** like **Tokyo Station** to ask which platform to go to.

When you need to read signs, menus, or product labels, the **image translation feature** is really helpful. Use it when you're in a **convenience store** like **7-Eleven** or **FamilyMart**, trying to figure out if a snack contains meat or dairy. Just point your phone's camera at the label, and it will translate the text for you. This feature is also useful in **train stations** like **Shinjuku** or **Kyoto** when you're using ticket machines that are only in Japanese.

If you're at a station like **Kyoto Station**, and you're confused by the signs, use the **camera feature** in Google Translate. Point it at the platform sign or ticket machine, and it will translate the text instantly. The same works in small restaurants around **Asakusa** or **Gion** when you can't read the menu—just scan it with your phone to know exactly what you're ordering.

These apps aren't perfect, so keep your sentences simple. Short, clear sentences are easier for the app to translate correctly. If you're asking for directions to **Meiji Shrine**, say, **Meiji Jingu wa doko desu ka?** The app will translate this clearly. Speak slowly and clearly to avoid mistakes. If you're going to areas with bad Wi-Fi, like **Hakone** or **Mount Fuji**, download the **offline language pack** before you travel, so you can use the app without internet.

If you're in **Shibuya Station** trying to find the exit for **Hachiko Statue**, just use the camera to scan the signs, and it will translate them for you. Or when you're at a small ramen shop and want to check if a dish has pork, use the voice translation feature to ask the staff directly. This way, you don't have to guess.

While these apps work well, they might mess up complex phrases, so it's a good idea to double-check important information. If you're using the **Shinkansen** from **Tokyo to Kyoto**, for example, and want to confirm your platform, use the app but also show your phone's translation to a staff member to make sure you're on the right track.

12.2.2 JAPANESE ETIQUETTE FOR FOREIGN VISITORS

When you're in **Japan**, being polite is a big deal. Whether you're in a busy spot like **Shibuya** or a quieter place like **Kyoto**, people really appreciate respect in every interaction. If you're at a **restaurant**, like having sushi at **Sushizanmai** in **Tsukiji**, or shopping at **Don Quijote** in Shibuya, say **"Arigato gozaimasu"** when thanking staff. It's better than just saying **"Arigato"** because it shows more respect, especially when you don't know someone.

Bowing is part of daily life. When you enter a **store** like **Uniqlo** in **Shinjuku**, you can greet the staff with a small bow and say **"Konnichiwa."** You don't need to bow deeply, just a little nod is fine. Bow again when you leave, saying **"Arigato gozaimasu"**. This goes a long way, especially in smaller places like family-owned restaurants in **Kyoto** or **Nara**.

If you're going to speak **English**, it's always polite to ask first. If you're at **Tokyo Station** asking for directions, you can start by saying **"Eigo o hanasemasu ka?"**, which means **"Do you speak English?"**. If they do, great. If not, keep your words simple or use gestures. For example, in a **restaurant** at **Ramen Street** in **Tokyo Station**, just pointing at the menu will help if the staff doesn't speak much English.

On **trains** or **buses**, like when you're riding the **Yamanote Line** in **Tokyo** or the **Shinkansen** to **Kyoto**, you need to keep your voice low. It's considered rude to talk loudly or take phone calls on public transport. You'll see signs reminding people to keep their phones on silent, especially in crowded places like **Shibuya** or **Shinjuku**.

When paying for something, like in a **shop** or **restaurant**, always hand over your money or card with **both hands**. You'll often see a small tray at the register, and you should place your money or card there. After they give you your change or receipt, take it back the same way. This is especially common in big department stores like **Takashimaya** in **Nihonbashi** or smaller shops in **Asakusa**.

In **Japan**, there's no tipping, so don't leave extra money on the table after a meal. If you've just had dinner at a nice spot in **Dotonbori** in **Osaka**, pay the exact amount, and say **"Arigato gozaimasu"** as you leave. That's all you need to do to show appreciation for good service. Personal space is important. In **crowded areas** like **Shibuya Crossing**, don't stand too close to people. When waiting in line, whether it's for the **metro** or outside **Asakusa Temple**, keep a respectful distance. If you need to gesture toward something, use your whole hand instead of pointing with one finger, which is seen as rude.

People here are generally more reserved with **gestures and facial expressions**. You won't see a lot of exaggerated hand movements or big reactions. So, when you're in quieter spots like **Nara Park** or walking around **Hokkaido**, it's best to stay calm and keep your gestures subtle.

12.3 NAVIGATING JAPANESE SIGNS AND MENUS

12.3.1 COMMON KANJI AND SIGNS YOU'LL ENCOUNTER

Traveling in **Tokyo, Kyoto**, or any other city, knowing some basic **kanji** will make navigating places much smoother, especially in busy areas like **Shibuya** or quieter spots like **Nikko**. If you're at a major station like **Shinjuku Station**, the first kanji you'll need to spot is 入口 (iriguchi), which means **entrance**, and 出口 (deguchi), meaning **exit**. These signs help you find your way in and out, especially in large, multi-level stations or crowded shopping centers. You'll see them on **platforms**, **buildings**, and **malls**, guiding you to where you need to go. If you're at **Narita Airport** or **Haneda Airport**, these signs will direct you to the correct areas for catching your next train or bus.

Once you're in a station like **Osaka Station**, where it can get confusing with multiple lines and exits, knowing 改札口 (kaisatsuguchi) for **ticket gate** helps you find where to scan your pass or ticket to enter and leave the station. This is especially useful during peak travel times, like heading from **Kyoto to Osaka** on the **Shinkansen**, where speed and efficiency are key. In **restaurants** or at train stations, you'll often need to find a restroom. The kanji トイレ (toile) or お手洗い (otearai) for **toilet** will guide you, and you'll often see them in places like **Tokyo's Ramen Street** or smaller eateries in **Asakusa**. Just make sure you know 男性 (dansei) for **men** and 女性 (josei) for **women** to avoid any awkward moments. You can usually spot these signs clearly at **stations** like **Shibuya** or **Kyoto**, as well as in major department stores like **Takashimaya** in **Nihonbashi**. To **menus**, understanding 魚 (sakana) for **fish** and 肉 (niku) for **meat** will make ordering food much easier, especially in local spots where English isn't common, like traditional sushi restaurants in **Tsukiji Market**. If you're at a famous ramen shop like **Ichiran** in **Shibuya**, these kanji will help you know whether the ramen contains pork (豚 - buta), chicken (鶏 - tori), or beef (牛 - gyuu). Knowing these characters also makes exploring smaller restaurants in places like **Gion** in **Kyoto** or food markets like **Nishiki Market** a lot more enjoyable, as you won't have to guess what you're eating.

Shopping is another area where kanji comes in handy. If you're walking around **Ginza** or checking out trendy stores in **Harajuku**, you'll want to know 営業中 (eigyouchuu) for **open** and 本日休業 (honjitsu kyuugyou) for **closed today**. These signs will let you know whether a store is ready for business, so you don't waste time walking up to a shop that's closed for the day. During sales, you'll see 割引 (waribiki), which means **discount**, plastered in shop windows—perfect for spotting bargains, especially during seasonal sales in areas like **Shinjuku** or **Osaka's Namba District**.

Another important kanji to recognize is 自動販売機 (jidouhanbaiki), which means **vending machine**. You'll see these everywhere—on street corners, in train stations like **Tokyo Station**, and even along the quieter streets of **Kyoto**. These machines offer drinks, snacks, and sometimes even hot meals for a quick refreshment while you're exploring. Prices typically range from **¥100 to ¥200** for drinks, making them an easy option if you're in a rush.

If you're exploring historic sites like **Fushimi Inari Shrine** in **Kyoto** or the beautiful **Meiji Shrine** in **Harajuku**, look for 非常口 (hijouguchi), which means **emergency exit**. Knowing this can be crucial when you're navigating large crowds or in case of an emergency, especially in popular tourist spots where many exits might be hidden.

Recognizing these kanji will make it easier to move around, whether you're trying to find your way out of **Tokyo Station** or ordering a dish in **Kyoto**. From street signs to menus, these characters are everywhere and being able to spot them quickly helps you enjoy your trip without stress.

12.3.2 HOW TO ORDER IN RESTAURANTS WITHOUT SPEAKING JAPANESE

If you are in a restaurant, especially in busy areas like **Shibuya** or **Asakusa**, and can't speak Japanese, the best method is to **point at the menu** or the **plastic food displays** that are often in the windows or at the entrance. These displays, common in places like **Osaka's Dotonbori** or **Kyoto's Gion District**, show exactly what the restaurant offers, and all you have to do is point and say **"Kore kudasai"** (This, please). You'll find this approach works particularly well in casual spots, whether you're having **ramen** on **Shibuya Center Street** or grabbing **takoyaki** near **Namba**. If there's a menu with pictures, use that to order— it's as simple as pointing to the photo of the dish you want.

In some smaller places, like hidden izakayas in **Nishiki Market** or traditional restaurants near **Arashiyama**, there might not be any pictures. But don't worry, the **point-and-order method** still works if you're in a spot where they display plastic food models at the entrance or the counter. For instance, in local ramen shops like **Ichiran** near **Shibuya Station**, the ordering system is often ticket-based, where you pick your meal from a vending machine, press the button next to the picture, and hand your ticket to the staff.

If you have **dietary restrictions**, you should be ready to communicate this clearly. If you don't eat meat, say **"Niku wa tabemasen"**, which means **"I don't eat meat."** This is useful when you're in areas known for specific dishes like **tonkatsu** (pork cutlet) in **Shibuya** or **yakitori** (grilled chicken skewers) in **Shinjuku**. Vegetarians can also look for dishes that include **"yasai,"** meaning **vegetables**. If you're allergic to certain ingredients, you can say **"Arerugii ga arimasu"** (I have an allergy) and point to the ingredient you can't eat using a **translation app** if needed. For example, if you can't have shellfish in a seafood restaurant near **Tsukiji Market**, use **Google Translate** to explain or show the waiter.

In tourist-heavy areas like **Ginza** or **Akihabara**, you can ask for an **English menu** by saying **"Eigo no menyuu wa arimasu ka?"** Many restaurants here, especially in places that see a lot of foreign visitors, will have an **English menu** available. In places like **Roppongi** or **Shibuya**, some restaurants may even have staff who can speak English and explain the menu to you. But even in areas without much English, like **Asakusa** or **Nikko**, you'll find that pointing to items on the menu or showing the staff the translated text from your phone gets the job done.

Getting to these places is easy, too, especially if you're using public transport. Most of these areas are close to **major train or subway stations**. For example, if you're heading to a ramen shop in **Shibuya**, you can take the **Yamanote Line** and get off at **Shibuya Station**. From there, it's just a few minutes' walk to **Shibuya Center Street** where you'll find plenty of dining options. In **Asakusa**, take the **Ginza Line** to **Asakusa Station**, and you'll be right in the heart of the district, where you can explore traditional food stalls around **Senso-ji Temple**.

One important thing to remember is that being **polite** when ordering goes a long way. After you order, when your food arrives, or when you leave, a simple "**Arigato gozaimasu**" (thank you) shows respect and appreciation, which is always welcomed by the staff. Even in busy tourist hubs like **Harajuku** or quieter places like the tea houses near **Fushimi Inari Shrine** in **Kyoto**, politeness and patience are key. The experience is always better when you show a bit of kindness and are open to trying new things.

CONCLUSION

.. And here we are. For the first, i would like to thank you so much for reading this wonderful guide. I really hope it helps you plan your Japan beautiful trip and makes things easier while you visit and absorb all the experiences. You have to know that I tried to include all the important information you'll need, so you can enjoy your time, even if you're traveling now or even in **2025**.

I'm new to writing, so I know there might be a few mistakes or things that could be clearer. For that, I'm sorry. If you spot any errors or if you have any questions, please feel free to email me. I would love to hear from you. And who knows, maybe someday we'll even meet in **Japan** while you're traveling. That would be really special!

Thanks again for choosing this guide. I hope you have an amazing trip and make wonderful memories!

Goog Luck!

Made in United States
Orlando, FL
13 December 2024